WILTON HOUSE

JOHN MARTIN ROBINSON

WILTON HOUSE

The Art, Architecture and Interiors of One
of Britain's Great Stately Homes

RIZZOLI/Electa

Contents

Foreword
The Earl of Pembroke

ON THE RUN-UP TO ITS 500-YEAR ANNIVERSARY, Wilton has been enjoying yet another renaissance in its long and occasionally turbulent history.

Since the early twenty-first century, almost all of the house interiors and adjoining buildings have been restored, renovated and redecorated under the careful and sensitive guidance of Victoria and me, along with our trustees, advisors, staff and contractors.

This follows a long and dedicated programme of restoration initiated by my father in the late 1980s that saw the complete renovation of the state rooms, the structural reinforcement of Wilton's South-East Corner, reroofing and electrical rewiring, among many other essential works.

Wilton is now in the finest condition it has been in for centuries, and as such was awarded the Historic Houses Association's "Restoration of the Year" in 2010 for the Dining Room, and went on to be recognised by the Salisbury Civic Society Conservation Awards for our restoration of the Holbein Porch and Triumphal Arch in 2016 and subsequently the Sawmill Bridge in 2018.

In recognition of these last three decades of intensive work, it felt only right to take this opportunity to record and mark all that has been achieved, not just over this period but over the lifetime of this magnificent house.

Wilton is first and foremost a family home, one that through the years has been architecturally shaped and moulded to evolve with the changes in style and fortunes of my family, and I'm sure you will delight in John's telling of this tale.

The arms of Bodenham, sixteenth-century stained-glass cartouche in the North Hall. The last abbess of Wilton was Cecilia Bodenham, pensioned off in 1539, when the Saxon abbey was dissolved by Henry VIII.

Introduction
The Medieval Past

WILTON HOUSE HAS BEEN FAMOUS FOR CENTURIES AS ONE OF THE MOST distinguished and beautiful country houses in Britain, and since 1544 has been the seat of the Herberts, Earls of Pembroke. In many ways it stands preeminent in English art history for its unique architecture, its Renaissance literary associations, its art collections and its Georgian landscaped setting. Wilton's aura is almost legendary: with architecture attributed to Hans Holbein (1497–1593) and Inigo Jones (1573–1652); the largest and oldest country house collection of antique Greek and Roman sculpture; and an unparalleled group of Old Master paintings and drawings with masterpieces by Raphael, Ribera, Holbein, Rembrandt, the Brueghels and Van Dyck; its cultural connection with Shakespeare, Philip Sidney, Christopher Marlowe and Ben Jonson. The "Wilton Myth", like the collections, is largely the work of Thomas Herbert, the 8th Earl of Pembroke, who inherited the estate in 1683 and died in 1733, and so reigned at Wilton for an amazing span of fifty years.

Thomas was the third son of the 5th Earl, Philip Herbert, who had completed the transformation of Wilton into a Carolean palace around 1652 and then received Cosimo III, Medici Grand Duke of Tuscany (1642–1723), there in 1669. Thomas, the 8th Earl, had inherited Wilton after the premature deaths of his two feckless older brothers who left the estate and house in a state of depletion, chaos and debt. Thomas determined to restore the fame and reputation of both Wilton and the Pembroke family. He was a brilliant publicist and very clever at what is now called public relations, surrounding himself with a "court" of younger writers, scholars and antiquaries, all of whom shared his knowledge and vision, and to whom he dictated the first guidebooks and the earliest art catalogues devoted to an English country house and its collections. First in manuscript or then more positively in print, these encapsulated Thomas's own understanding of Wilton, and created an immortal legend that has persisted to this day, constantly repeated in histories, guidebooks and art and topographical literature.

Thomas, the 8th Earl of Pembroke, saw himself as the heir to Thomas Howard, the 14th "Collector" Earl of Arundel, the "father of vertu in England", in Horace Walpole's phrase, and Wilton under the 8th Earl was intended to compete with and surpass Lord Arundel's Tudor Inigo Jones Arundel House in the Strand, London, and to revive and perpetuate the cultural glories of the Stuart Court and the English Renaissance. Lord Pembroke's self-identification with Arundel was cultural, but there was also a family connection. William, the 3rd Earl of Pembroke, had married Mary Talbot, daughter of the 7th Earl of Shrewsbury and sister of Aletheia, spouse of the "Collector" Earl of Arundel, though they had no children. Lord Arundel certainly visited his brother-in-law at Wilton and was there in 1615 when he told his wife that James I was due to stay shortly.[1] This was a tenuous link, and the whole compact Stuart peerage was otherwise interconnected by marriage. Lord Pembroke saw himself as Arundel's successor as both a collector and a patron. He liked to think that his statues and pictures came from the Arundel Collection. As Peter Stewart demonstrates in the catalogue of Wilton's sculpture, there is no historical evidence that the 8th Earl acquired any statues directly from the Arundel Collection[2], though some of the items in the Mazarin Collection may have belonged previously to Arundel or Charles I. Old Master drawings and paintings acquired by Pembroke from Sir Peter Lely also included works previously owned by Arundel, but that too was at one remove. The idea that Lord Pembroke acquired significant portions of the Arundel Collection directly, and the provenance of the art, armour and sculpture at Wilton, is partly myth, invented by the 8th Earl himself. This misrepresentation is also the case with the story of the building's architecture.

Pembroke claimed that the 1st Earl's new Tudor house at Wilton was designed by Hans Holbein, the most famous artist at the Court of Henry VIII, and that the classical south front and state rooms, the apotheosis of a Stuart Court style, were the unaided achievement of Inigo Jones, Charles I's architect. "The Earls of Pembroke had from the reign of Henry VIII been encouragers of the fine arts, and very early showed their taste in employing Holbein and Jones in improving and adorning their noble seat at Wilton", wrote James Kennedy in the frequently reprinted eighteenth-century guidebook to Wilton. It was based directly on information originating from the 8th Earl. As Kennedy put it: "In this work are introduced the Anecdotes and Remarks of Thomas Earl of Pembroke, ... now first published from his Lordships MSS"[3].

Drawing attributed to Wenceslaus Hollar of Wilton House, *circa* 1635. The gabled tile-roofed houses behind show how closely the town abutted the north-west side, as indicated on the survey plan.

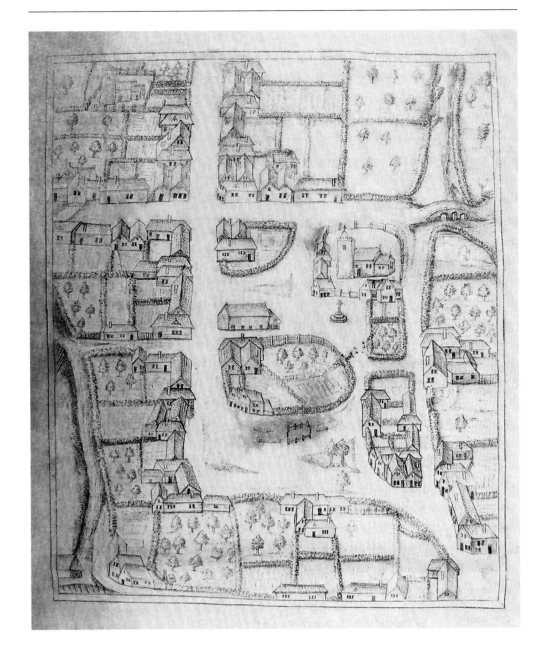

Plan of the town of Wilton from the 1st Earl's estate survey, 1563–65, showing St. Mary's Church, the old rectory and the marketplace. The abbey, and site of the present house, was situated just off the bottom right-hand corner.

The "anecdotes" of the 8th Earl, however, contained a degree of wishful thinking, and were not entirely accurate. Holbein had died in 1543, the year before the full grant of the Wilton estate to the 1st Earl, and before the construction of the new house. So he could not have been involved in its design even though the "Holbein Porch" is a masterpiece of English Renaissance architecture. The heraldic decoration on the porch and elsewhere on the 1st Earl's house dates its architecture firmly to after 1551 and the bestowal of the Earldom of Pembroke. It was the work of two leading Tudor mason-craftsmen, Thomas Collins and John Chapman, the former a special protégé of the 1st Earl. As will be shown, although the 4th Earl's reconstruction of the house was definitely Jonesian and Inigo Jones was involved, the new facade, state rooms and formal garden were the joint work of a much wider team of Stuart Court artists and craftsmen, albeit all part of the Jones stable, including

[27]

Isaac de Caux, John Webb, Nicholas Stone and Edward Pearce, whose role in the decoration has been underestimated.

Wilton House is not a uniform architectural masterwork like Holkham, Houghton, Hatfield, Blenheim, Burghley, Hardwick, Kedleston, Osborne, Belvoir and so many of the major English houses, but rather the opposite: an accumulation of alterations and additions over many centuries. There have been three major phases of architectural reconstruction as well as piecemeal alterations between the sixteenth and twentieth centuries. But the "Wilton Myth" has been an important factor in the development of the house into its present form. The work of previous generations was respected by successive owners. The basic plan and character of the 1st Earl's mid-sixteenth-century house has been retained. The 4th Earl in the

opposite The Holbein Porch. Long attributed erroneously to Hans Holbein, the porch was the feature of the 1st Earl's house most admired by subsequent generations; however, it dates from the 1550s, after Holbein's death.

seventeenth century admired the "Holbein Porch". The 11th Earl and James Wyatt in the early nineteenth century went out of their way to keep everything they thought was by Hans Holbein or Inigo Jones. This approach persisted into the twentieth century when a conscious attempt was made to meld the different parts into a harmonious whole, respectful of the perceived history of the place, which is not the least interesting aspect of the Wilton story.

Wilton as it exists today forms a compact square with two– or three–storeyed ranges of ashlar stone and four corner towers. It was developed out of medieval monastic buildings surrounding an inner court, and stands on the footprint of a

above Aerial photograph from the south, showing how the plan of the present house is dictated by the claustral plan of the abbey with four ranges around an inner court. The church was probably sited under the present south front.

700-year-old nunnery suppressed during the Reformation. To this day it retains the claustral plan of the post-Norman rebuilding of a Saxon foundation. The retention of the quadrangular plan of its abbatial predecessor was deliberate on the part of the 1st Earl of Pembroke in the 1550s. A courtyard house with medieval feudal associations remained the grandest form of house plan for a noble seat in the sixteenth century, and even into the eighteenth century when centralized Palladian plans had become the norm, as demonstrated at the 4th Duke of Bedford's impeccably classical Woburn, or even the 11th Duke of Norfolk's Georgian Gothic Arundel with axial enfilades round a "Quadrangle". Those plans/buildings were intended as demonstrably ducal palaces and not "villas". The 1st Earl of Pembroke's Wilton was an evocation of medieval lineage, in its plan and towering gatehouse, as well as its sophisticated courtly Renaissance classicism. The latter style showed the earl's understanding of up-to-date metropolitan fashions, while the corner towers, the inner courtyard and the gatehouse harked back to the castle style evocative of the late Middle Ages, and military chivalry. It was the architectural equivalent of Lord Pembroke's Milan and Greenwich-made armour, warlike but engraved and gilt with Renaissance filigree decoration.

The property acquired by the 1st Earl, in two grants in 1541 and 1544, had been a house of Benedictine nuns for nearly seven hundred years. The history of the convent is given in a fifteenth-century poem preserved in the British Library, but how reliable that is about the early centuries is doubtful.[4] Some sort of religious foundation was established at Wilton, then the capital of Wessex, at about 800. Alburga, sister of King Edgar of the English, persuaded the king to make it into a priory of nuns of which she became the abbess in 830. King Alfred expanded it in 890, to house twenty-six nuns. Certainly there was a religious house at Wilton by 934 when King Athelstan made it a grant of land. It was a royal foundation for nuns of noble birth, with a school for girls. King Edgar's daughter, Edith, had been a pupil there and her mother abbess. Edith spent much of her life at Wilton, the church being rededicated to her after her death and her canonisation as a saint. She was obviously a strong character, as indicated by her well-known response to St. Adelwold when he reproved her for her fine dress: that she in her garments of gold thread could be just as virtuous as he in his filthy animal skins. After her death, her tomb became a shrine in the abbey church and was repaired and embellished by Edward I in the thirteenth century.

The original buildings were of timber, but were reconstructed in stone in the eleventh century. The stone-built new church, erected by the wife of Edward the Confessor, was finished and consecrated by the Bishop of Sherborne and Ramsbury (the predecessor of Norman Sarum) in 1065. Although the convent had large estates, its status as a royal foundation and resulting links to the king imposed heavy financial responsibilities, including paying for five knights in the king's service, and looking after royal "boarders" nominated by the king and queen. Following the Norman Conquest, Wilton's abbess, like Shaftesbury's, held her lands directly from the king through feudal tenure by knight service. Wilton, with Shaftesbury, Winchester and Barking, was one of the four greatest nunneries in medieval England.

Nevertheless the convent faced intermittent financial difficulties from the thirteenth century onwards, and received outside help from time to time. In 1256, Henry III granted oaks for repairing the church and house, and the Treasurer of Salisbury Cathedral gave money for the church. It is likely that the buildings as reconstituted in the mid-thirteenth century and repaired after a fire in the fourteenth century survived until the end of Wilton as a convent. By the time of its dissolution, the place was described as being in a "ruinous" state, though thirty-three nuns still lived there, and the income was computed by the king's commissioners at £700 per annum, the fourth largest of any convent in England. Much of the wealth came from wool and sheep farming. The abbey was surrendered to Henry VIII on the same day as King Alfred's other foundation of Benedictine nuns at Shaftesbury in Dorset, March 25, 1539. The last abbess, Cecilia Bodenham, was granted a generous pension of £100 and a house at Fovant to the south of Wilton, and all the nuns were given annuities graded according to seniority.[5]

The abbey buildings with most of the estates, comprised of land in all the surrounding parishes, were granted to Henry VIII's brother-in-law Sir William Herbert (the future 1st Earl of Pembroke) in two grants, in 1541 for his lifetime, and in 1544 to Herbert and his successors in perpetuity. The first grant was to "William Herbert, Esquire and Anne his wife for the term of their lives" with certain reserved rents. The 1544 grant was explicitly "to the aforementioned lord, by the name of Sir William Herbert, Knight, and the Lady Anne his wife and the heirs male of their bodies between them lawfully begotten." The appearance of the old religious buildings is not recorded, but references in medieval documents indicate there was a dormitory, hall, chapter house, infirmary, hospice and of course a church. In the later Middle Ages, the abbess also had her own independent residence, and her own courthouse because she ranked as a baron and had rights of justice in the locality, as well as her religious functions, and her role as a great landowner.[6]

William of Worcester, the fifteenth-century antiquary and traveller recorded after a visit that the church contained "90 of my steppys" in length while the width of the nave with its flanking aisles was "46 of my steppys". No one knows how much William of Worcester's footsteps measured, but comparison with buildings described by him elsewhere and that still exist suggests that the Wilton church, or at least its nave, measured 146-feet long by 72-and-a-half-feet wide, which compares in scale with the church, for instance, at Malmesbury Abbey.[7] It would have been oriented with the high altar and nuns' choir to the east, but it is not known for certain on which side of the cloisters the church was situated. Most modern writers have assumed that it was on the north side as was the general case with monastic plans. But no foundations or traces have been discovered. It is just as likely that it was on the south side flanking the river, not on the town side where other buildings came up close to the north range. The sculpted remains of a late twelfth-century doorway with elaborate decoration were uncovered in 1992 under James Wyatt's Gothic Stairs at the south end of the east range and are likely to have been part of the church building. It is similar to the processional door surviving at Lilleshall Abbey, Shropshire, which gave access from the cloister to the church there. This

following pages The Gothic Hall designed by James Wyatt in 1803. The 11th Earl's adoption of the Gothic style in the early nineteenth century was a Romantic-era attempt to restore Wilton's medieval abbatial appearance.

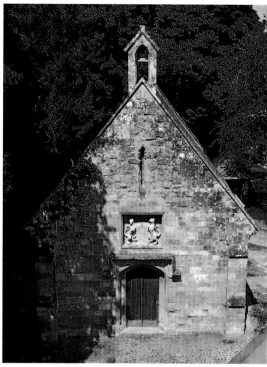

above left The Almonry. Originally twice its present length, this range is the principal surviving medieval building on the site and retains several late-Gothic windows. The name is a corruption of armoury, to which use it was converted by the 1st Earl. Its original function is not known.

above right The south gable of the Almonry. The bell cote was added to the medieval structure by James Wyatt.

opposite Tudor doorway surmounted by a shield of medieval arms. The arms are made up of fragments. The rampant (standing) panther and lion are the supporters of the Pembroke arms. The shield, with a lily symbolising virginity, is that of the abbey, dedicated to St. Edith (a Saxon princess).

similarity would support the view that the church at Wilton was on the south side of the cloister, not the north. There are parallels for such a plan in Wiltshire at Lacock and Old Sarum, where the churches were on the south side of the cloisters. Recent archaeological excavation at Wilton's sister foundation of Shaftesbury has discovered that the church there was on the south side of the cloisters and not, as thought in the 1930s, on the north. This reinforces the supposition that the Wilton church was on the south side too. The known layout of the Tudor house with the Great Hall on the north side and the Long Gallery on the west, suggests that these succeeded the refectory and dorter in the same positions. The 1st Earl's house with Great Hall on the north, gallery on the west, gatehouse tower on the east and great rooms on the south still determines the layout of Wilton today.

The Wilton Myth states that the monastic buildings were demolished, with the exception of the large fourteenth-century barn at Washern, across the River Nadder, to the south, and the "Almonry", a single-storeyed medieval range of unknown purpose to the north-west of the present house, and salvaged medieval stone was used to build the new house in the 1540s. It is more likely that only the church was demolished, though bits of it may have been incorporated in the Tudor south range, and the monastic buildings round the cloisters were retained and remodelled, as at Lacock in Wiltshire. Repairs at different times in the twentieth century have revealed that this was the case. Work after dry rot to the north wall of the south wing in 1947 showed that it was medieval for almost its full height on the courtyard side; also, a new door to the Single Cube Room cut-through revealed a medieval embrasure at today's first-floor level. The west wall of the Single Cube Room is also medieval with the remnant of a moulded door embrasure on the ground floor below.

Underpinning and restoration in 1991–92, preceded by archaeological research in 1988,[8] revealed medieval stonework at the south-east corner. The north and east fronts still show substantial areas of medieval masonry of local sandstone from Hurdcott (three miles west of Wilton), notable for its greenish tinge and harder quality than the creamier Chilmark Stone used from the sixteenth to the eighteenth centuries. Eighteenth-century plans of the house depict considerable discrepancies in the thickness of some of the inside walls, suggesting the retention of old fabric, especially at the north-west corner. All four sides therefore retained pre-Tudor work. Adaptation of the residential abbey buildings would have made practical sense, and parallels the policy of the 1st Earl's contemporaries and Wiltshire neighbours: Sir William Sharington at Lacock, who kept all the buildings except the church there, and Sir William Thynne at Longleat (in the first phase of building), also an ex-religious house. Surviving monastic fabric, as well as the courtyard plan, still determines the character of Wilton.

The present house, reconstructed out of the medieval abbey and the 1st Earl's quadrangular Tudor house is, however, visually a seventeenth-century and Georgian creation. Only the great East Gatehouse tower stands *in situ* as a demonstrative Tudor element, the Holbein Porch now being a garden feature. Otherwise the south and east fronts present tranquil Palladian elevations to the world, relying on classical proportions with a *piano nobile* over a basement storey, understated astylar Vitruvian window architraves, cornices and crowning balustrade; emphasis is provided by four taller pedimented corner towers of Scamozzi derivation, and the sculptural centrepiece of the south front in the form of a Venetian window or "Serliano", an avowedly royal architectural declaration. It is this serene classical image, the combined work of Inigo Jones and Isaac de Caux, which established an

Washern Grange, barn interior. The large fourteenth-century barn is an impressive survivor of the medieval abbey and is situated in the park across the River Nadder, where there was once an independent hamlet.

admired archetype for the eighteenth-century English country house. The south front was the backdrop when built to an elaborate formal garden with parterres, fountains and a grotto, now all smoothed and transformed into an idyllic, designed Georgian landscape with cedars and the magical eighteenth-century Palladian bridge designed by Henry, the 9th "Architect" Earl of Pembroke, as an eye-catcher crossing the River Nadder, which flows through the park. The south front was rebuilt in 1636–47 by Philip, the 4th Earl of Pembroke, Lord Chamberlain, at the suggestion of Charles I especially to receive the king on his summer progress. The interior of that range comprises a royal state apartment for the reception of the king, magnificently decorated to the design of Inigo Jones, John Webb and Edward Pearce, with gilded wall carvings, inset portraits by Anthony Van Dyck, and painted ceilings. These rooms are the finest surviving interiors from the Stuart Court, and they remain the special architectural glory of Wilton, unique in English architecture for their self-assured palatial quality.

In the early nineteenth century, the house was further remodelled by James Wyatt (1746–1813) who ingeniously rearranged the interior to create a comfortable and practical Regency house plan. He added the picturesque Gothic Cloisters with plaster rib vaults around the inner court in tribute to Wilton's abbatial past and also to serve as sculpture galleries for the display of Wilton's unique assemblage of antique Roman sculpture. Finally, in 1913, the north front was remodelled by the young and fashionable Edwardian architect Edmond Warre as an ingenious synthesis of Wilton's architectural history, combining elements of Tudor and Inigo Jones-inspired derivation to create an appropriate artistic overture to Wilton's multi-faceted architectural splendours.

Washern Grange. Exterior of the medieval barn with stone buttresses dating from the late fourteenth century.

Wilton House from the south-east. A classic image showing
the mid-seventeenth-century south front, the palladianised
Tudor east front with the 1st Earl's Gatehouse, and the
9th Earl's Palladian Bridge of 1733 that crosses the River
Nadder, all set amidst cedar-studded lawns.

The east front and entrance forecourt created by the 1st Earl, an ink
sketch from the 1563–65 survey. The central gatehouse tower survives.
The outer gatehouse was removed in the early eighteenth century.
The pediment was replaced with a parapet by James Wyatt, but the
general disposition of the Tudor flanking wings and corner towers
still underlies the later classical remodelling.

Chapter One
The Tudor House

WILLIAM HERBERT, CREATED IST EARL OF PEMBROKE IN 1551, RECEIVED THE
abbey buildings and surrounding lands from the crown, and adapted medieval
monastic Wilton to form a splendid quadrangular Renaissance house. Herbert had
a remarkable career – the model of a successful Tudor courtier, despite a dodgy
beginning. Having become "an esquire of the body to the King" (the king's armour-
bearer) in 1526, a junior post in the household, obtained through the influence of
his father, Sir Richard Herbert, a Gentleman Usher to the king, he threw away this
opportunity by stabbing a man to death in an affray in Bristol. He then had to flee
back to Wales, where the Herberts originated and where his father had some inherited property.

   Herbert returned to London about seven years later after a period of obscurity,
and married Anne Parr in 1534, the younger of two daughters of Sir Thomas Parr
of Kendal, Controller of the Household to Henry VIII. In July 1543, Anne's elder
sister Catherine became the sixth queen of Henry VIII. Thomas Herbert found
himself the brother-in-law of the king. Royal favour was showered on his wife and
on him. He was knighted in 1543 and in January the following year was appointed
captain of the town and castle of Abergavenny, reinforcing his influence in Wales.
In the spring of 1546, he became a Gentleman of the Privy Chamber, close to the
person of the king, and was granted the keepership of Baynard's Castle on the
Thames at Blackfriars, which became his London house. He was also appointed
steward of royal property in the west of England and granted Cardiff Castle and
the crown lands attached to it in Glamorgan; the grant of Wilton Abbey was
confirmed to him and his wife and their descendants in 1544. This was a substantial augmentation of the landed property in Wales and the west that he had begun
to accumulate in the 1530s with a lease of Abergavenny Priory and its estates. It
was a spectacular reversal of his youthful fall from grace. His success owed a lot
to his military prowess. "A mad fighting young man", John Aubrey (1626–1697)

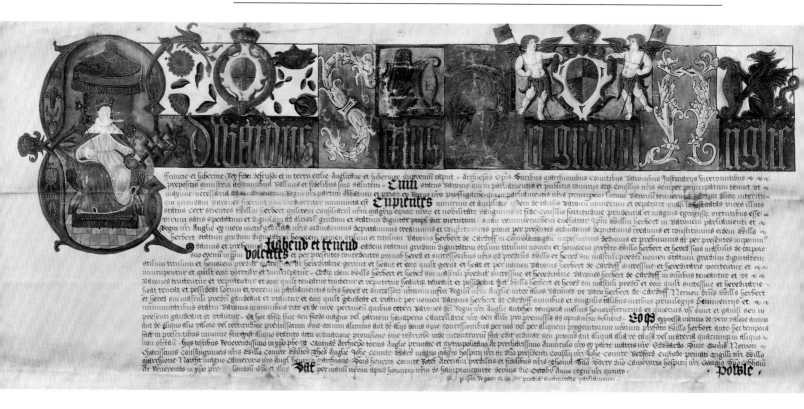

Illuminated vellum patent of the grant of the Earldom of Pembroke to William Herbert by King Edward VI in 1551.

called him, and this trait of character was valuable when diverted from brawling to the king's service. Hotheaded but shrewd, energetic and warlike, with a likeable manner, he was to become the chief military commander in Tudor England and remain in favour during four reigns, those of Henry VIII, Edward VI, Queen Mary and Queen Elizabeth. His lands in Wiltshire, Glamorgan and the Marches established him as one of the most powerful landowners in the west. He made his fortune in the dangerous waters of the Tudor Court, benefitting from the fluid market in church and crown lands: "His disposition got favour and his prudence wealth". He was the English equivalent of an Italian condottiere, important in light of Henry VIII's military ambitions in France, and intermittent need to suppress civil strife at home. Welsh estates were crucial to the 1st Earl's military standing. While not as profitable as arable land in eastern England, or the rich wool pastures of Wiltshire, the estates provided him with fighting men and influence; traditionally the king's armies were heavily dependent on recruiting archers and other soldiers from the Welsh Marches. For instance, in 1544, Herbert was able to put together a troop of one hundred light horsemen under his own command for the Boulogne campaign in France, while he accompanied Henry VIII as the king's squire and armour-bearer. Henry VIII's Italian armour from that occasion was preserved as a trophy at Wilton for three hundred years. Herbert built up a large private armoury at Wilton composed of pikes, swords, staves and bows for a company of fighting men, as well as gifts of royal armour and splendid suits of damascened steel for himself. He was first and foremost a military commander.[1]

Herbert was proud of his ancestry and applied for and received a regrant of the Herbert arms in 1542 (with a bordure for difference, dropped by his son); the illuminated vellum patent survives at Wilton today. The Herberts were a Welsh Marcher family who had first become nationally prominent in the fifteenth century. Sir William Herbert, who died in 1446, bought Raglan Castle in Monmouthshire. His son, also William, was a Yorkist in the Wars of the Roses and supported Edward IV. He was summoned to Parliament as Lord Herbert in 1461, and in 1468 was made Earl of Pembroke of a new creation by Edward IV. He then fell victim to the Lancastrian backlash in 1469 and was captured at Northampton by Henry VI's army and beheaded. He left one legitimate son, also William, born in 1455 who succeeded as 2nd Earl but exchanged that title at the king's request for the Earldom of Huntingdon. He only had one daughter, Elizabeth, who married Sir Charles Somerset, later Earl of Worcester and ancestor of the Dukes of Beaufort. Elizabeth as an heiress took Raglan and the Herberts' Monmouthshire estates to her husband's family when her father died in 1491.

The Yorkist Earl of Pembroke also had an illegitimate son, Richard, who was the father of William, the 1st Tudor Earl of Pembroke, and the builder of Wilton House. Richard Herbert had to make his own way, though he inherited a small landholding in Wales. Like many Welshmen, he took advantage of the Tudor dynasty's capture of the throne at Bosworth in 1485 to pursue a career at court in London. He became Gentleman Usher to Henry VII and later Constable of Abergavenny Castle. He laid the foundations for a new Pembroke dynasty that William Herbert was able to build on with such success.

Following the death of Henry VIII in 1547, William became an executor of the king's will and received a personal legacy of £300. He was in a strong position during the reign of the boy King Edward VI: Chief Gentleman of the Privy Chamber, member of the twelve-strong Privy Council, and Master of the Horse, first supporting Thomas Seymour, Duke of Somerset, and then John Dudley, Duke of Northumberland, successively the king's de facto regents. William Herbert's military command was useful in 1549, when he suppressed the rebels in Wiltshire and Dorset who were protesting against enclosure, religious change and general

Portrait of William Herbert, 1st Earl of Pembroke, *circa* 1560. He wears the collar of the Order of the Garter, which he was granted in 1549, and holds his white wand of office as Lord Steward of the Royal Household.

economic ills. He was made a Knight of the Garter in the same year. He attached himself to John Dudley, Earl of Warwick and Duke of Northumberland, who succeeded the Duke of Somerset as guardian of the young king and effective ruler. Although Northumberland soon followed Somerset to the scaffold, William Herbert profited from the association, and his architecture was influenced by Dudley's. In 1551, Edward VI created him Earl of Pembroke. In the 1550s, Pembroke was several times Lord President of the Council of Wales and was Lord Lieutenant of Wiltshire from 1551 to his death in 1570. In 1552, the new earl entertained the boy king at his rebuilt house at Wilton, an occasion recorded by the Royal Arms of Edward VI being

Frontispiece from the *Survey of Lands of William Earl of Pembroke*, commissioned in 1563 and completed in 1565. The ink drawing shows the 1st Earl seated and receiving the auditors responsible for the survey. The Italianate ornamental borders and heraldry echo the decoration of the 1st Earl's house.

proudly displayed over the main entrance in the impressive new East Gatehouse, suggesting that the principal part of Wilton House was reconstructed by then, or at least in that reign.

As a Protestant, Lord Pembroke did not welcome the succession of Queen Mary Tudor and briefly supported Lady Jane Grey, but rapidly changed tack when he saw that Mary had popular support. He continued to serve her, as he did Elizabeth I, under whom he became Lord Steward of the Household. His major military victory was ironically in the reign of Mary when he defeated the French outside Calais at the Battle of St. Quentin.

The 1550s, which saw the high point of Pembroke's fortunes, is the most likely date for the creation of the new house at Wilton, though the documentation is sparse and detailed building accounts do not survive. The 1563–65 survey, however, stated that the 1st Earl "newly constructed all the houses, gardens, orchards and other appurtenances at a cost of £10,000" and this notation gives a *terminus post quem*. At the time of Pembroke's initial lifetime grant in 1541, it is unlikely that he would have embarked on an ambitious scheme to create a lavish new seat. The grant in perpetuity in 1544 would have given the security for a grander scheme, as would the acquisition of the borough of Wilton, and the forest of Groveley from the crown, giving him total dominance of the locality. Comparison with Lacock and Longleat suggests that there were probably two phases of development, an initial reduction and adaptation of the convent buildings to make a secular residence, and then an ambitious project to create a new Renaissance mansion on a grand scale. The latter is more likely to have taken place in the 1550s than in the 1540s, and is dated by the heraldry, both the arms of Edward VI as king and by Pembroke's own arms as an earl, with peer's supporters and coronet.

The main task immediately after acquisition of the abbey would have involved the removal of the church. The demolition of a church on the scale of Malmesbury Abbey or Old Sarum Cathedral, removing the rubble and dressing stone for reuse, would have taken a year at the very least, possibly two building seasons. The abbey church at Barking in Essex, for instance, which was admittedly of larger size, took nearly two years to demolish in 1541–42, and to remove its materials. In Sussex, Lewes Priory took one year to destroy with a large workforce. Comparison with Longleat, which is contemporary and unlike Wilton well-documented, is instructive. The present grand mansion is largely 1570s, but there were two earlier phases. The first took three years, from 1546 to 1549, and formed a residence in Tudor style round a single courtyard, fashioned out of a convent of Augustine Canons. It was small compared to the present mansion at Longleat. A second phase, from 1553 to 1556 added new lodgings, the hall and a stone porch. The work at Wilton paralleled it. The distinguished mason-designer John Chapman was involved at this stage in both houses.

Chapman was a stone carver and had a high reputation. He had been employed in the King's Works in London since around 1541. He was consulted by several noblemen as well as the court in the 1550s. He was known to Sir William Cavendish in Derbyshire and the Parrs at Sudeley Castle, Gloucestershire; made a chimneypiece for Dudley Castle for the new Duke of Northumberland, and worked for William Sharington at Lacock in Wiltshire. After the execution of Northumberland in 1553, he worked at Sir William Thynne's Longleat House in Wiltshire for several years, carving heraldic beasts on gable ends and working on the new porch, where he carved the arms of Thynne and the Duke of Somerset, for whom Thynne had been secretary. Chapman's contract of 1559 preserved in the Longleat archives mentions doorcases, beasts, chimney crests, chimney columns, "terms" and great windows. He was paid 10 pennies a day for his work, which was influenced by the new Strand front of Somerset House, in such Renaissance details as the support of the windows on classical corbels and the use of Doric friezes and Doric columns and pediments. Somerset House was also distinguished for one of the earliest English classical pediments. Several of the London craftsmen who worked at Somerset House also worked at Longleat, including Allen Maynard, the sculptor who produced three carved chimneypieces. There was a fire at Longleat in 1567 that led to even more ambitious building between 1568 and the 1570s, when the existing facades were added, but it was the 1550s and 1560s work involving Chapman and Maynard that paralleled the 1st Earl's reconstruction of Wilton and, though documentary evidence is lacking, it is likely that they too worked for the 1st Earl of Pembroke at the same time.

The Holbein Porch is almost certainly by Thomas Chapman, on the strength of the parallels with his lost Longleat porch and the deployment of heraldry and literate classical detailing. The porch can be dated by the heraldic evidence to after 1548, when Lord Pembroke received the Garter shown encircling his three escutcheons of arms on the front and sides of the porch; it can be dated even later, to after 1551, when Pembroke received his peerage, as the full arms on the front include an earl's coronet and peer's supporters. The porch was in existence before 1563, when the survey of Lord Pembroke's estates (completed in 1565) was begun and shows the east front in an ink drawing, and describes the house as completed. That survey also gives some rare hard evidence for the building work at Wilton. Under the manor of Burcombe, it is recorded that "Also within this same manor be fair young wooddes of v or vj yeares, conteigning by estimacion xvj acres, all which wooddes are now felled spent and consumed … [for] burning of Lyme aboute the Lords buyldings at Wilton".[2]

This account reinforces the likelihood that Lord Pembroke created the new mansion at Wilton in the 1550s, after he was given the Garter and earldom, and it was probably planned around the time of Edward VI's visit in 1552, although not completed then but certainly before the compilation of the estate's survey, which records it in 1563–65. It is a celebration of his noble status and his closeness to the sovereign.

The Holbein Porch is two-storeyed, constructed of fine-grained Bath limestone of highest quality, with a band of dark grey marblelike material, "touchstone", for the entablature between the two storeys. This indicates the polychrome nature of the original design, still attested by traces of sixteenth-century pigments in green, black, gold, red and blue. The design comprises a literate double order of fluted Ionic columns on the ground floor with Corinthian above, with accurate mouldings and

The Holbein Porch. Conceived as the main entrance into the Great Hall from the courtyard. Removed by Wyatt and reconstructed in the west garden in 1826, it was the work of the mason-architect Thomas Chapman, inspired by Sebastiano Serlio.

The 1st Earl's arms. The shield depicts the quartered Herbert arms, with supporters, coronet, crest and garter. The arms date the porch to after 1551 and the creation of the earldom. The flanking roundels depict Apollonius of Tyre and his wife, from classical literature, a Renaissance idea.

architraves. The parapets are formed of mini segmental pediments of semicircular shell or fan shape supporting carved stone putti and heraldic beasts as finials, similar to those provided by Chapman at Longleat. Somerset House scroll corbels appear both in the upper entablature and as support for the stone roof inside (which was also painted in colours, gilded and decorated with foliage). There are no windows, and the upper walls on all three sides display rectangular panels framed with exquisite guilloche and egg-and-dart mouldings framing richly carved heraldry of the Herbert arms, all encircled by the Garter. The principal heraldic display on the front also shows numerous quarterings, supporters, coronet and crest.

The arms are flanked by circular niches containing busts, often said to be family portraits, but are, in fact, figures from classical literature as indicated by weathered inscriptions identifying Apollonius Prince of Tyre and "Laoite" possibly Lucina his wife. Apollonius was the hero of a late classical romance that was popular in the Middle Ages and Tudor period. An English translation by Robert Copland was published in 1510, and was obviously known to the 1st Earl and his circle. This sculpture emphasises the serious classical nature of the sophisticated design, and the fine quality of the stone carving belies the image of the 1st Earl as a rough-and-ready soldier, devoid of learning or taste, as do the musical instruments, books and luxurious writing box listed in his 1562 inventory. The porch is a significant work of art in terms of carving, classical design and polychrome decoration and proves that Tudor Wilton was a magnificent piece of Renaissance architecture.

The porch – Chapman's masterwork and the focus of the courtyard – was notable for its assured Italianate detail with correctly proportioned classical orders of two tiers of columns: Ionic over Corinthian with correct architraves, mouldings and entablatures derived from engravings by Sebastiano Serlio (1475–c.1554). According to Aubrey the porch was even admired by Inigo Jones himself, who described it "as good architecture as any was in England".[3] The influence of Serlio demonstrates how the 1st Earl's architectural taste was affected by his political and Protestant allegiances; the Protector Duke of Somerset at Somerset House, before his execution, Sir William Thynne and his building campaigns at Longleat; Sir William Sharington at Lacock; and John Dudley, Duke of Northumberland, who led the government of Edward VI from 1550 until his execution in turn in 1553. Dudley, in particular, an admiral and competent statesman, had an interest in Italian Renaissance architecture and was a patron of John Shute (d. 1563) whose book *The First and Chief Grounds of Architecture* was the first treatise in English on classical architecture. Dudley paid for Shute to visit Italy in 1550 and study at first hand the works of "ye skilful maisters in architecture". Dudley had commissioned a new residential wing at Dudley Castle built by Chapman under the supervision of Sir William Sharington of Lacock. This was one of the earliest examples of the influence of the Italian Renaissance on an English country house. Shute came back from Italy with sketches, which were not

The Royal Arms of Henry VIII. Beautifully carved in Bath Stone like the Holbein Porch, this panel is attributed to Thomas Chapman. Inset by Wyatt over the north front entrance, these arms probably came from the demolished outer gatehouse which stood before the 1st Earl's east front.

published until 1563, but were shown at court, and Lord Pembroke would have been aware of them and Shute's description of the classical orders. The Holbein Porch was the product of this knowledge amongst a group of pioneer classical patrons and builders, with which Lord Pembroke was closely associated, and his house at Wilton has to be seen in this precocious architectural context.

Related to the Holbein Porch is the carved panel of the arms of Henry VIII, which was reset on the north front by James Wyatt in 1809. The Royal Arms, too, are carved with virtuoso skill in Bath Stone, comparable to the porch, and different from the Chilmark Stone used for most of the new building at Wilton; they have traces of polychrome paintwork like the Holbein Porch. They show the quartered arms of England, three leopards *passant guardant* quartered with France Modern, three fleur-de-lis, and vigorous supporters: a crowned lion and a fierce griffin, encircled by the Garter and surmounted by the royal crown. The background is prettily carved with scrolls and Tudor roses and the king's initials H.R. The whole achievement is supported on another pair of Somerset House scroll brackets. The original position of this carving is not known, but it may have been on the elevation of the outer gatehouse where a heraldic panel is shown on the 1565 survey, and it would have preceded the arms of Edward VI over the main archway on the gatehouse tower, emphasising the source of Lord Pembroke's good fortune. This splendid sculptural achievement of the Royal Arms is probably by Chapman and was carved at the same time as the porch between 1551 and 1563. It was therefore a retrospective tribute by the 1st Earl to his royal benefactor after the king's death, just as Edward VI's arms on the East Gatehouse tower commemorated that monarch's continuing royal patronage with the bestowal of the earldom, and visit in 1552.

The towering East Gatehouse was the most impressive external feature of the 1st Earl's house and the major recognisable architectural element still extant. It, too, shows the influence of Somerset House and was originally topped with a wide classical pediment, an early appearance of such a classical element on a large scale in England. It was the principal feature of the east side of the house, forming the main entrance with an open archway on the ground floor. Such a gatehouse harked back to late medieval practice as well as Tudor palaces like Hampton Court. The original appearance of the east front is shown in the sketch in the 1563–66 survey. The gatehouse is four storeys high with large mullion and transom windows and survives largely intact, though sensitively altered by James Wyatt around 1803. Wyatt extended the first-floor mullion windows on the east elevation downwards to accommodate the replanning of the internal floor levels at that time, and as a result he moved the carved panel of Edward VI's arms up a storey, from the base to the top of the projecting bay window. Wyatt also replaced the pediment with a high parapet displaying four carved sixteenth-century panels of the Pembroke arms, two on each face, which were removed when Wyatt's Cloisters were built, and re-set in the top of the gatehouse. This heightening aimed to maintain the dominance of the central gatehouse when the side links were raised a storey by Wyatt. The extant corner towers of Scamozzi-Palladian influence repeat the scale of their Tudor predecessors which were gabled with ornamental chimney stacks.

The East Gatehouse. It survives as built by the 1st Earl, though the crowning parapet was added by Wyatt, who also extended the first-floor mullion windows of the central bay downwards to suit his rearranged internal floor levels. The Royal Arms of Edward VI record the bestowal of the earldom in 1551, and the king's visit to Wilton in 1552. They date the structure.

[51]

Although its two lower storeys are screened by the Cloisters, the east elevation of the gatehouse is the best preserved with original mullion windows, carved gadroon stringcourse and a pair of magnificent sixteenth-century lead downpipes moulded with classical lions' heads and strapwork decoration derived from the engravings of Hans Vredeman de Vries. It gives a good indication of the 1550s appearance of the inner courtyard, which sported a similar carved stringcourse all round, and regularly arranged mullion and transom windows. The handsome, regular elevations of the courtyard made that space into the principal feature of the external architecture. In the 1st Earl's house the windows of the main rooms looked into the courtyard, and the fewer windows in the outer south, west, and north sides were irregular and the surrounding walls retained medieval fabric, an arrangement that survived on the north and west sides until Wyatt's reconstruction after 1800.

The main entrance through the four-storeyed tower on the east side was preceded by a deep, rectangular outer court that measured 168-feet wide and 390-feet deep. The area was entered through a smaller two-storeyed outer gatehouse 49-feet high and flanked by turrets with onion domes, and the little central gable over the archway was topped with the Pembroke Wyvern crest. This outer gatehouse was demolished in the early eighteenth century by the 8th Earl of Pembroke, but is illustrated in the 1563–65 survey, and still survived at the time of the Grand Duke of Tuscany's visit in 1669.

The east front and the inner courtyard were the two principal architectural features of the 1st Earl's house, forming a grand interrelated entrance procession. The general form of the quadrangle has survived later alterations, and the two major accents, the gatehouse and the Holbein Porch are also extant, though the latter is now *ex situ*, having been carefully dismantled and rebuilt in the west garden as an eye-catcher in the early nineteenth century. Conceived as the main[4] entrance

below left The Royal Arms of Edward VI on the gatehouse. These form a pendant to those of Henry VIII. Well carved in Bath Stone, they are also likely to be the work of Thomas Chapman, *circa* 1552.

below right Sixteenth-century lead downpipes on the Gatehouse. The embossed decoration with lions' heads and strapwork is derived from engravings by the Flemish artist Hans Vredeman de Vries, a popular source.

The inner face of the East Gatehouse. The well-preserved mullion windows and the carved gadroon stringcourse give an idea of the architecture of the 1st Earl's inner courtyard.

to the house from the inner court, it was positioned off-centre on the north side, leading to the screens passage at the bottom of the Great Hall.

Drawings of 1803 by J. C. Buckler show the porch *in situ* and the north side of the courtyard, the mullion windows by then replaced with sashes, but the sixteenth-century gadroon stringcourse still running around the elevation, matching that surviving on the gatehouse.

Buckler showed that the north side of the courtyard was two-storeyed with a high blank parapet. Investigations during restoration work in 1988–92 revealed that the south elevation opposite was three-storeyed with a second floor of lodging rooms above the main apartments on the first floor, all with mullion and transom windows (still extant, blocked, behind Wyatt's Cloisters). The Tudor "great apartment" was on the first floor on the south side, an arrangement which survives to the present day, though the rooms there now face outwards to the south.

Sir Roger Wilbraham, Solicitor General in Ireland, kept a journal of his travels round the country between 1593 and 1616, and visited Wilton when the 1st Earl's house was intact, on a day out from Salisbury. He noted the feature of the inward-looking rooms and courtyard windows. "The Earle of Pembroke hath 2

[53]

miles off a faire house called Wilton, a large and high built square of hewen stone: the rooms having ther lightes but one way into the square are melencholick and dark".[5] The rooms may have been dark, but the courtyard itself was full of sunshine on a fine day, and its sculpted classical and heraldic decorations were painted in a rich polychromy, including the shields of arms. Modern research has uncovered traces of red, blue and green colours, and extensive gilding on the carved stonework, especially on the Holbein Porch, as has been noted.

The interior of the 1st Earl's house has disappeared entirely, but an idea of its character can be gleaned from contemporary descriptions and inventories. It was as impressive as the courtyard and east front with tapestry-hung rooms and magnificent chimneypieces of varied stones and marbles. The principal rooms, following the monastic layout, were largely on the first floor, and at least, in part, the medieval vaulted undercrofts survived on the ground floor in the sixteenth century.

From written descriptions certain features of the Tudor interior – notably the chimneypieces – were comparable with surviving contemporary work in Bristol, where several merchants' houses had rich plaster ceilings and elaborate chimney-pieces with large overmantels. For this work, another of the 1st Earl's protégés may have been responsible, Thomas Collins (d. 1594), a leading mason carver. He was brought from London by Lord Pembroke, for whom he had worked at Baynards

right J. C. Buckler's watercolour, 1803, of the Holbein Porch before its removal by James Wyatt to make way for the Cloisters. The parapet and gadroon cornice from the 1st Earl's courtyard survived until that date, though the windows were sashed to replace mullions in the early eighteenth century.

opposite The East Front. The Tudor composition is perpetuated in Palladian dress. The 1st Earl's house was not a new building but a reconstruction of medieval monastic fabric, as demonstrated by the survival of green-tinged Hurdcott sandstone, as opposed to the Chilmark Stone largely used at Wilton from the sixteenth to the nineteenth centuries.

[54]

Portrait of the 1st Earl, School of Hans Eworth. The woven rush matting and the "Spanish" armchair hint at the interior furnishing of Tudor Wilton House.

Castle in Blackfriars.[6] After Lord Pembroke's death in 1570, Collins moved to Bristol where he became a Freeman in 1571 and was the principal mason-architect-carver in the city during the latter part of Queen Elizabeth's reign. In Bristol, Collins was responsible for some important houses, including the Red Lodge for William Young, the Collector of Customs, a job owed to Lord Pembroke who was Constable of Bristol Castle and Steward of the city.

The character of Lord Pembroke's lost Tudor interior of Wilton is captured in a contemporary inventory of the contents, and also in a written description before Carolean reconstruction by Lieutenant Hammond, an officer of the military company in Norwich who travelled to the west of England in 1635 and visited Wilton then. Hammond's first name is not known, but he was obviously educated as he understood Latin and law. In records he comes across as jovial and friendly with antiquarian interests and "High Church" sympathies. He visited Wilton at the moment the seventeenth-century formal garden was being created, but before the 4th Earl's renovation of the house between 1636 and 1647; his is, therefore, a record of the Tudor interior in the last decade of its existence. He described the house as "stately and prince-like", and gave the names and sequence of the main rooms, whereas the 1558–62 inventory lists the contents in kind and does not mention all the rooms where the items were housed. The references to the king's arms embroidered on beds shows that much of the furnishing must have been made around the time of Edward VI's visit in 1552, and the inventory is partly based on notes dating from 1558. With its long lists of spectacular textiles, the record gives a good impression of the luxury of the 1st Earl's interiors, with elaborate beds, rich hangings, tapestries and upholstery worthy of a royal palace:

In my Lordes Chambre a rich tester with the valance and base paned with blewe tisseue clothe of red and grene bawdkin and grene velvet and silver imbrodered with the Kinges armes, a quilte belonging to the same, V courtens and a beddstedd. A rich tester of crimson velvet imbrodered with my Lordes armes, double valance to the same, V courtens of double sarcenett, colour redde and a beddstedd to the same.

Fifteen other beds of equivalent grandeur were listed with cloth of silver, murrey and white satin, gold lace, and green velvet hangings; two of them were also embroidered with Lord Pembroke's arms. The grandest was "A riche tester paned with golde and redde velvett imbrodered with the Kinges armes, double valance to the same, V courtens of red and yellowe damaske, a quilte of the same imbrodered with the Kinges armes". There were also six rich canopies of velvet and gold lace that were not attached to bedsteads, and forty-two "riche quiltes", some of them coverings for tables. Sixty-seven cushions of velvet, satin and tissue, with gold and silver lace were also listed. There were thirty-nine upholstered chairs, some of them "Spanish fashion", some with "my Lordes armes" and some with other embroidered decoration, including flowers and the "scallop shell". There were also two "Cloase stooles covered with red cloth of golde", another of "redde velvet" and two of "wrought black velvet", the epitome of luxury, and no doubt intended for Lord and Lady Pembroke's and the king's own use, and that of special guests. There were also eleven chamber pots. In addition to the splendid upholstered chairs intended for the state rooms and principal bed chambers, there were also forms and stools with upholstered seats of velvet, tissue and silk; the long forms would have been for the hall (as at Oxford or Cambridge) and only the Pembrokes and the king would have had chairs at high table. Nineteen "cloth" or Turkish carpets were listed, and these were covers for tables and cupboards rather than floor coverings. Judging from Lord Pembroke's portrait, the floors had woven rush matting.

The dominant element in the rooms was the wall hangings. These varied from gilt leather to paned damask, but were principally "arras", or tapestry. The leather hangings composed a set of twelve pieces, "gilte with my lordes armes". These may have been in Lord Pembroke's Drawing Room. The tapestries included verdure and poetry but were predominantly biblical subjects. They ranged from a set of nine pieces and two "chimneypieces" (panels to go over a fireplace) of David and Joseph, through several sets of eight pieces, of the stories of Hester, "Toby", "Jacob", to smaller sets of the story of Tobias, David, "Jeromy". There were also four different sets of the story of David, another of seven pieces of Samson, a single "chimney piece" of Hester, "the rest being at London", indicating that some sets were split between Wilton and Baynards Castle. The only classical set comprised eight pieces depicting the story of Romulus and Remus. The near ubiquity of biblical subjects is interesting. One two-piece set displayed heraldry: "hangings of red clothe with the hartes hedde and the Stafforde knott". Altogether twenty-two different sets of hangings are recorded which suggests that all the principal rooms were hung with tapestry and luxury textiles.[7]

The chapel had two especially splendid "hangings of rich arras with golde of the Passion". The almost popish grandeur of the chapel is apparent from the inventory and is particularly striking in view of the often repeated view that Lord Pembroke shared the strong Protestant views of the Somerset circle. On the contrary, he seems to have foreshadowed the rather "High" conservatism of Elizabeth I's chapels royal. There were altar cloths of red velvet and silver, murrey caffa, green caffa, green damask, blue damask fringed with silver and red silk; ten copes of cloth of gold, white damask, blue silk, black and red caffa, green caffa embroidered with gold, and two copes of red caffa. This makes an almost complete set of the medieval liturgical colours for different seasons and feasts. In addition, there were "paires of vestiments" of cloth of gold, cloth of silver, and white damask, and single vestments of green and blue caffa "mingled with golde", yellow caffa, "changeable caffa", "blewe and redde caffa" and green damask. There were also listed remnants of "coapes of gold" and "borders that was coapes of golde and dyvers colours of silke" that sound as if they were pre-Reformation salvage. The chapel was obviously an impressive interior situated among the principal rooms.[8]

Not surprisingly, in view of the 1st Earl's military prowess, was the inclusion of an armoury at Wilton. It formed a major feature of the Tudor house. It was 180-feet long and was housed in one of the surviving medieval buildings. Aubrey said it was in a monastic structure, possibly a "dorter". This is the building now called the "Almonry" to the north-west of the house, its modern name being a corrupt memory of the 1st Earl's adaptation of an older building to display his magnificent collection. (The Almonry is shorter today, having been damaged by the fire in the seventeenth century and truncated.) Reflecting its importance, the armour was listed in detail in the 1558–62 inventory.

Lieutenant Hammond corroborates the evidence of the inventory; as a soldier the armoury was foremost in his attention and received more detailed description than the main rooms.

There was one thing more that I desir'd to see, of which I had heard a great report, to see which was well worth a Journey taking only, both for richness, and service, and (setting aside that great Storehouse of the Kingdome the Tower) it may well compare with any in the Kingdome. That is a most gallant Armoury which is 60 yards in length, the number of Armes therein will completely furnish, and fit 1,000 Foot and Horse: brioles, 30. Staves, 30. Welsh Hookes, 60. Black Bills, 20. Holy Water Springers around 60. Staves which were weapons to guard the old Lord's Person, with many other Offensive, and Defensive Armes as Coats of Maile, etc. At the further end of this Armoury, in a little Partition by itselfe, are some special rich Armes, and of great esteeme, viz Henry 8th and Edward the 6th, their Armes, The Lord William Herberts who was this Lord's grandfather, who wonne the town of St. Quintin in France, which was his Raysing.

Half suit of damascened steel parade armour by Pompeo della Cesa of Milan, a survivor of the once larger collection of sixteenth-century armour made in Greenwich and Milan, which furnished the 1st Earl's armoury at Wilton.

The Lord Henry's his Son, richlie gilt, inlayed, and graven with his Coat of Arms, from head to foote, which cost a good pretty summe the Ransomings King Henry 8th Armour Bearers Armes richlie gilt; Two Knights Armes Millain gilt; King Henry 8th Leading Staffe and his warlike Scepter; the Lord William his Turkish Scymister or Sable, wherewith he fought at St. Quintin, and his whole Armour for his horse richly graven and gilded.[9]

According to the Wilton Myth, the armour was captured from the French commander, Anne de Montmorency. Constable of France, by William, the 1st Earl, at the Siege of St. Quentin. In fact, as correctly recorded by Hammond, the gilt-black, steel armour was made in Italy for Henry VIII in 1543 and given to Pembroke as the king's squire and armour-bearer. It is now in the Metropolitan Museum of Art in New York.[10]

The 1st Earl's armoury at Wilton was the most extensive and impressive military collection in an English country house. It survived complete until the mid-seventeenth century, but Aubrey tells us the working arms and armour were taken in the English Civil War. The family trophy armour, however, survived at Wilton as one of its treasures until it was sold in the early twentieth century. It is represented today only by three pieces, one of the Milan knight's armours and two reacquired English breastplates redisplayed in the North Hall.

Portrait of the boy King Edward VI, who re-created the earldom of Pembroke for William Herbert in 1551 and visited Wilton House in 1552.

Hammond's description of the main rooms is revelatory and with the aid of the structural evidence, enables the plan before Inigo Jones and John Webb to be understood. Hammond was shown round by the housekeeper's young sister: "First she shew'd me the Gallery, richly hung … next through a neat withdrawing room into the Earle's Bed-Chamber, which was most richly hang'd. The Chamber next the Garden, call'd the King's Chamber the Hangings therein being Cloth of Gold, and over the Chimney Piece is the statue of King Henry 8th richly cut, and gilded over. Next was I shew'd the King's withdrawing Roome and the Billiard table Chamber, next the Chappell, both richly hung. The Great Dyning Chamber, very richly hang'd, in it is a most curious Chimney Piece of Alabaster, Touch-stone and Marble, cut with

Carved stone heraldry commissioned by Henry, 2nd Earl of Pembroke, in the 1570s.
centre A panel of the quartered Pembroke arms with the earl's coronet, one of a series displayed originally in the inner court but removed to make way for the Cloisters and resited by Wyatt at the top of the East Gatehouse.
left The arms of the 1st Earl of Pembroke, Herbert quartered, with supporters, nobleman's helmet and garter, on the south aedicule added *circa* 1570 to the Gatehouse.
right The arms of the 2nd Earl of Pembroke, Herbert quartered, with supporters, nobleman's helmet and garter on the north aedicule, added by the 2nd Earl to the gatehouse.

opposite Elizabethan heraldic stained glass commissioned by Henry, 2nd Earl of Pembroke, in the 1570s, probably for the Great Hall at Wilton; installed by Wyatt in the new Cloisters windows in 1806, under the direction of Maria Eginton. *Top left* King Henry VIII; *top right* King Edward VI; *bottom left* 1st Earl of Pembroke; *bottom right* 2nd Earl of Pembroke.

several statues, the King's and his Lordship's own Armes richly sett out: All the rest of the Chimney Pieces, are very rich, and faire." From a neat rich chamber "where I pleas'd my gentle She Guide" Hammond descended to the "fayre Great Hall, and stately 4 square built Court, beautify'd about with the King's and his own Armes" and entered the new garden on the south through "the archt cellars".

This description is illuminating. The Tudor Great Hall was on the north side of the court entered by the Holbein Porch, and remained there until remodelled by James Wyatt in 1809. The Gatehouse on the east side interrupted the floor levels, which would have prevented the creation of a long gallery in that situation. It seems likely, therefore, that the gallery was on the west side, perpetuated by the gallery-like succession of parade rooms in the eighteenth century, and now Wyatt's Library. The King's Bedroom, Hammond confirms, was definitely on the south side adjoining the gardens, as were presumably the succeeding rooms in his description. The Tudor great apartment, therefore, occupied the same position as its Inigo Jones and John Webb successors with the King's Drawing Room foreshadowing the Double Cube. The chapel would seem to have been at the south-east corner, lit by the large mullion and transomed window at first-floor level shown in the 1563–65 survey drawing. The demolition of the Tudor chapel, if it was in the place needed for the King's Dressing Room (the Corner Room) in the 4th Earl's replanning, would explain why it became necessary to build a new chapel at the other end of the house for which Isaac de Caux (1590–1648) prepared a design in about 1640.[11] Hammond's description implies that the dining room was on the first floor, and it was no doubt in the equivalent position to the chapel at the north end of the east wing, in the balancing tower, adjacent to the Screens passage of the Great Hall and conveniently near to the kitchen, which was housed in an independent structure to the north of the main house. Detached kitchens were a medieval convention to reduce the risk of fire, as at Glastonbury or Durham. So it is possible that the 1st Earl's kitchen was a monastic survival retained for

its usefulness. Medieval foundations were excavated in that area in 1988.[12] The kitchen remained a semidetached structure on the site, unaligned on the quadrangle, and approached by a covered way until Wyatt's alterations in 1809.

The 1550s house survived until Philip, the 4th Earl of Pembroke's classical reconstruction in the 1630s and 1640s. The 2nd Earl, Henry, who succeeded his father in 1570, while not making substantial alterations, embellished the building and park. He was responsible for the two Elizabethan aedicules on either side of the east gateway on the lower storey of the entrance tower. They are of Chilmark Stone and are not keyed into the masonry behind. Their Flemish mannerist decoration is derived from the engravings of Hans Vredeman de Vries (1527–1607), a popular source for Elizabethan architectural decoration. The aedicule to the south of the arch has a large escutcheon of the much quartered arms of the 1st Earl, encircled by the Garter, and the one to the north has an even more extensively quartered display of his own arms also encircled by the Garter. These armorial achievements are part of a large-scale display of heraldic decoration inserted throughout the house, both in carved stone and stained glass, and distinguishable from the 1st Earl's work by the use of Chilmark rather than Bath Stone. Six carved escutcheons of the Pembroke arms, re-set by Wyatt at the top of the gatehouse and on the bases of the two oriels on the east and west sides of the Cloisters form part of this scheme. They originally decorated the inner courtyard which Lieutenant Hammond noted was "beautify'd about, with the King's and his own arms".[13]

The heraldic stained glass comprised a planned programme of cartouches of the Pembroke and the Parr family arms, the Royal Arms from Henry VIII to Queen Elizabeth I, and those of Tudor Knights of the Garter connected to the Pembrokes as relations or political allies. The armorial glass would originally have embellished the rooms, especially the Great Hall windows, following standard Elizabethan practice, as still to be found, for instance, at Deene Park in Northamptonshire. The glass was restored and the Royal Arms extended from James I to George III by Maria (Wyatt) Eginton and reset in the Cloisters windows for her cousin James Wyatt in 1807, but still forms an important display of Elizabethan heraldic window decoration.

Heraldry was a strong interest of the 2nd Earl's: Aubrey tells us that he was a patron of men of learning, scholars and antiquaries, and was responsible for the heraldic decoration: "Henry Earle of Pembroke was a great lover of heraldrie, and collected curious manuscripts of it, that I have seen and perused; eg the coates of armes and short histories of the English nobility and books of genealogies; all well painted and writ. 'Twas Henry that did sett up all the glasse scutchions about the house".[14]

Henry, the 2nd Earl, shared his scholarly and literary interests with his brilliant wife, Mary, sister of Sir Philip Sidney who wrote *Arcadia* at Wilton and dedicated it to her. Highly educated and fluent in several languages, she, in particular, was the focus of a "dazzling literary court", a leading patron, and herself a distinguished writer, translating the Psalms into English. Mary Pembroke posthumously published her brother Philip's works after he was killed at the Battle of Zutphen in

Holland. She and Henry made Wilton into a centre for the arts and sciences, paying pensions to literary figures, antiquaries and others. Wilton was the model of a Renaissance Arcadia, where the arts and learning flourished in a pastoral setting. Aubrey called it an "academy".

Lord Pembroke had his own Company of Players that performed plays by Shakespeare, Thomas Nashe and Ben Jonson. According to the Wilton Myth *As You Like It* had its "first night" at Wilton. Lord Pembroke's players were also the first to perform *Henry VI Part 3* in 1599. Shakespeare is one of Wilton's adopted cultural heroes. The First Folio was dedicated to the "incomparable brethren", Lord Pembroke's sons William and Philip, who succeeded in turn as 3rd and 4th Earls. And William Herbert, the later 3rd Earl, is the most plausible candidate for the "W. H." of the sonnets. Other writers in the group assembled by Mary Pembroke were John Donne and Edmund Spenser.

The scientists and explorers in Wilton's cultural gatherings included Adrian Gilbert, the half-brother of Sir Walter Raleigh. Gilbert had a reputation as an alchemist and gardener and advised on laying out the garden at Wilton. He was a great favourite of Mary, Countess of Pembroke, and lived at Wilton for a time while working with Lord Pembroke on improvements to the garden and park. He was responsible for the impressive brick and stone Roman-style wall bounding the south side of the park, across the River Nadder. Mary and Henry also laid out Sir Philip Sidney's Walk, a level allée of lime trees with views north over the park to the house. Their principal surviving contribution to Wilton was the two-tier Italianate marble fountain erected in the inner court around the time of their marriage in 1577. The lower bowl is carved with the Sidney crest, a bristling porcupine. The fountain, now in the Italian Garden on the west front, is the principal survivor from the 2nd Earl's time and is a memorial to Wilton's cultural golden age.

Queen Elizabeth I visited Wilton in 1574, and occupied the gilded and tapestried great apartment that the 1st Earl had created for Edward VI. The queen was "merry and pleasant". Henry met her carriage five miles from Wilton, "accompanyed with … a good band of men in their livery coates, who also lined the two courtyards for the Queen's arrival at the house".[15] It was a triumphant show piece occasion. Tudor Wilton bathed in the royal approbation. James I visited in similar state in 1603, which may have been the occasion of the performance of *As You Like It*, but despite three further visits from the king during his life, it was thereafter deemed that Wilton was not grand enough for Stuart monarchs, leading to a radical rebuilding in the next reign.

above Elizabethan fountain of white marble erected in the central courtyard by the 2nd Earl, *circa* 1577, to commemorate his marriage to Mary Sidney. The bottom bowl is carved with the porcupine crest of the Sidneys and the Wyvern crest of the Herberts, marking the union of the two families.

following pages The east side of Wilton in dawn light, capturing the remarkable beauty of the house and setting.

Chapter Two
Atelier Inigo Jones

THE FAME AND IMPORTANCE OF WILTON HOUSE DERIVES PRIMARILY FROM THE seventeenth-century south front and the state rooms within. The design of these parts has always been associated with Inigo Jones, though their authorship is complicated. More ink has been spent on interpreting and describing the design and provenance of this phase in the development of Wilton House than on almost any other historic English house.[1] The picture that emerges from a sequence of studies by Howard Colvin, John Summerson, John Harris, Alan Tait, Gordon Higgott, Giles Worsley, John Heward, John Bold of the Royal Commission on Historic Monuments and other scholars is now generally clear. All the surviving documentary evidence has been trawled and sifted and interpreted, and the fabric itself explored in archaeological and structural investigations in 1988–1992.

The generally agreed conclusion is that Inigo Jones was indeed involved but worked through assistants, chiefly Isaac de Caux who designed the south front and garden in the 1630s, and John Webb who reconstituted the state rooms from 1647 to 1652, after fire damage. The work was all done with the oversight of the royal architect, Inigo Jones; only Jones's exact responsibility for elements of the design remains debatable. As it exists, the south front is a truncated version of a larger scheme intended to have a central portico. Giles Worsley and Howard Colvin considered the unexecuted grand portico design for the south front to be by Jones, while others have attributed it to Isaac de Caux.

The executed design is definitely based on a drawing by de Caux at the RIBA. The corner towers not shown on that drawing were probably suggested by Jones, inspired by Palladio's pupil Scamozzi, whom Jones had met in Venice. Various other subtle refinements of the design, including the flat quoins added to define the corner towers, also not shown on the de Caux elevational drawing, were likely suggested by Jones. The neat termination and breaking forward of the top cornice at either end

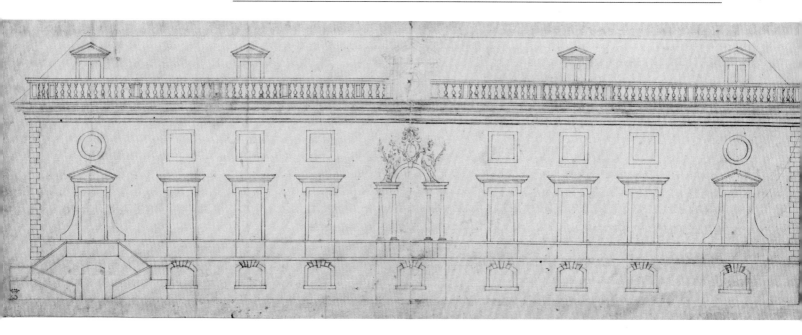

above Isaac de Caux's design for the south front, without the flanking tower pavilions. It is a truncated version of Inigo Jones's grand design for Wilton and only half its width.

of the façade so that it emphasises the two towers, are subtle classical details that also show the hand of Jones. Nitpicking over the precise contribution of different artists, however, misses the point of the Carolean rebuilding, in that the 4th Earl of Pembroke himself was not just the patron who commissioned the project, but also the driving aesthetic force behind it. It is his artistic vision that was realised at Wilton between the 1630s and his death in 1649, and it reflects his own cultural experience and architectural taste. In particular the new Wilton has to be seen in the context of Lord Pembroke's official visit to Paris in 1626, when he escorted Princess Henrietta Maria of France to England as bride-to-be of Charles I, and was housed at the new Luxembourg Palace just as it was being decorated by Queen Marie de Medici in advanced Franco-Florentine taste. The interior design made a dazzling impact on the visiting earl. The character of Wilton's state rooms with their heavily gilded ornament, inclusion of painted decoration as an integral part of the architectural scheme and large marble chimneypieces reflects Lord Pembroke's own taste – derived from his personal experience of that contemporary Parisian palace by Salomon de Brosse, which established seventeenth-century French classical style. Lord Pembroke's own interiors at Wilton survive, whereas the seventeenth-century rooms at the Luxembourg were replaced in pompous nineteenth-century *style officiel* when it was converted into the seat of the French Senate in the 1850s. The contemporary source of Lord Pembroke's inspiration for his new palace at Wilton is not as obvious now as it might have been if Marie de Medici's interiors had survived for comparison's sake. Daniel Defoe (who had travelled on the Continent) compared Wilton to the Luxembourg. Philip, 4th Earl of Pembroke,[2] was a metropolitan figure, and a man of culture and taste who had spent his whole life from youth onwards in the Stuart Court in the ambiance of Queen Anne of Denmark, Henry, Prince of Wales, Charles I, and Queen Henrietta Maria, all of them sophisticated patrons of the arts and architecture, even if Philip had initially risen to favour through the attention of

left Gilt statuette of Inigo Jones, by Richard Westmacott, *circa* 1820, after the statue by Michael Rysbrack at Chiswick House, a Regency tribute to Inigo Jones, seen by successive generations as the architectural hero of Wilton.

Anthony Van Dyck. *Portrait of Queen Henrietta Maria.*
The 4th Earl, as Lord Chamberlain, visited Paris in 1626 and escorted
the future queen back to England to become Charles I's bride. In Paris,
the earl stayed at the new Luxembourg Palace, designed by Salomon de
Brosse for Marie de Medici, which was the inspiration for the spectacular
seventeenth-century, Franco-Florentine state apartments at Wilton.

top The Stables at Wilton, designed
by Isaac de Caux, seen here as originally
built in a painting of *circa* 1700, hanging
at Wilton House. The Stables adjoin the
barn at Washern Grange.

above The Stables today, with
the open arcade blocked to make
cottages. The design lacks the
finesse of Inigo Jones.

the less aesthetic James I, and owed his original advance to his skills at dancing and sport. But his love of hunting was equalled by a discerning taste in painting, such as sharing Inigo Jones's enthusiasm for Parmigiano.

Born in 1584, Philip was educated at New College, Oxford (like his elder brother Thomas), but soon moved on to London, seeing his best future, as the younger son, at court where his youthful good looks, sporting prowess and civility soon earned favour, and he was created Earl of Montgomery in his own right and given lucrative sinecures by James I. He continued to be in favour in the next reign and was appointed Lord Chamberlain by Charles I in 1626 (the year after the king's accession), in charge of the royal palaces, a position he held until 1641 and the outbreak of the English Civil War. He was not as learned as his elder brother William, the 3rd Earl, who had been Chancellor of the University of Oxford and a benefactor of the Bodleian Library, to which he had presented 250 Greek manuscripts from the Barocci Library in Italy and was described by Anthony Wood, the Oxford historian, as a "person truly generous, a singular lover of learning ..."

William, 3rd Earl, had no children and on his death in 1630 the Earldom of Pembroke passed to Philip who became a double earl. Philip also had literary and artistic interests, as well as a passion for the country and field sports. He was a collector of paintings and a leading patron of Anthony Van Dyck, and also contemporary writers. Authors dedicated more than forty books to him during his lifetime. After his inheritance, Wilton then became the focus of his life. He maintained a household staff of one hundred and fifty, larger than the household of eighty at Durham Place in the Strand, his new London house replacing his grandfather's at Baynards Castle. He also had a grace and favour court residence as Lord Chamberlain at Whitehall Palace, which remained the site of the London house of the Earls of Pembroke until 1827.

There is strong evidence that Philip personally directed the building work at Wilton. For instance in 1647–48, he refused to leave Wilton House to attend the debate in the House of Lords on the "Vote of No Addresses" aimed at breaking off parliamentary negotiations with Charles I. He gave as his reason that he was attending on the rebuilding of new state rooms following a fire. This absence also reflected Philip's political wish for a compromise between the king and Parliament at the end of the First Civil War and his wish not to take sides publicly, despite having become a moderate parliamentarian. His excuse of the

Anthony Van Dyck. *William Herbert, the 3rd Earl of Pembroke*. William and his brother Philip were the "incomparable brethren" to whom Shakespeare dedicated the First Folio of his plays. The painting is one of the full-length portraits in the Double Cube Room.

renovation was considered plausible by his contemporaries, and indicates that his personal role in the works at Wilton was recognised by them. The state rooms were created under his own on-site supervision until his death in 1649.

At Wilton Lord Pembroke established a regular pattern in the 1630s, entertaining the king every summer. This annual Royal Progress was the impetus for the reconstruction. Work began with the garden in 1632, and the new south front of the house itself was undertaken from 1636. It is built of brick, faced in Chilmark ashlar; brick faced with stone was a construction technique developed in the Office of Works at this time. When Lt. Hammond visited Wilton in 1635, the garden was well underway. The instruction by Lord Pembroke to rebuild the south front is dated the following year in March 1635–36. As Lord Chamberlain, he issued a personal warrant "to take down … that side of Wilton House which is towards the Garden and such other parts as shall be necessary and rebuild it anew with additions according to the Plott which is agreed".[3] That Lord Pembroke gave this in his own official capacity, rather than through his estate steward at Wilton, or an architect, is another indication of his personal direction of the rebuilding at Wilton. Tree-ring-dating of timber in the south front shows that the trees used were felled in 1636–37, giving the exact date of the rebuilding work. The genesis of the design is outlined by John Aubrey, the Wiltshire writer, antiquarian and neighbour who knew the place well and got his information at first hand. He stated that Charles I "did love Wilton above all places and came thither every summer … It was he that did put Philip … Earle of Pembroke upon making this magnificent garden and grotto, and to new build that side of the house that fronts the garden, with two stately pavilions at each end and all al Italiano. His Majesty intended to have it all designed by his own architect, Mr. Inigo Jones, who being at that time, about 1633, engaged in his Majesties buildings at Greenwich, could not attend to it, but he recommended it to an ingenious

The south front as executed, *circa* 1700, from the painting attributed to Leonard Knyff, showing the simplified formal parterre centred on the west pavilion tower, after the truncation of the grand design, the north towers still with tiled caps not pediments. The stone staircase descending from the Hunting Room to the grounds was removed by the 9th Earl of Pembroke around 1733, when he landscaped the garden.

architect, Monsieur Solomon de Caus, a Gascoigne, who performed it very well; but not without the advice and approbation of Mr. Jones".[4]

Howard Colvin first pointed out that this reference must mean Isaac de Caux, as the older Solomon had gone to Heidelberg to design the Elector Palatine's garden by the 1630s. Isaac de Caux had worked with Jones on the design of Covent Garden for the Earl of Bedford, for whom he also remodelled Woburn Abbey where his grotto survives. Jones himself was fully occupied in the 1630s with the design and building of the Queen's House, Greenwich, the surveyorship of St. Paul's Cathedral, and a whole series of elaborate court masques, of which he was designing two a year; he had enough on his hands without getting involved in a new building project in Wiltshire.

Inigo Jones had known Wilton from earlier visits when James I commissioned him in 1620 to investigate Stonehenge, which he thought to be Roman. Jones's Stonehenge project was published posthumously by his architectural pupil and nephew-in-law John Webb. Lord Pembroke had worked with Jones previously when, along with his elder brother the 3rd Earl and the Earl of Arundel, he was one of the commissioners who organised James I's funeral in 1625. Inigo Jones had designed the domed catafalque, "the fairest and best fashioned that had been seen".

above The south front with the west pavilion today with the stairs removed.

following pages Anthony Van Dyck. *The Great Family Piece* (detail). The painting fills the west wall of the Double Cube Room and shows the 4th Earl, his wife and children in front of a cloth of estate framed by fluted columns, making a grand dynastic statement, with the earl's quartered arms. Lord Pembroke wears the collar and Great George of the Order of the Garter, and the ornamental key symbolic of his role as Lord Chamberlain.

[75]

Engraving of the formal garden designed by Isaac de Caux, 1632, before the south front with the grotto at the end of the central axis. From *Hortus Pembrocianus*, *circa* 1640.

As Lord Chamberlain to Charles I, and senior court official he was directly responsible for all the Jones-designed work in the royal palaces at Whitehall, Greenwich, Oatlands, Somerset House, Newmarket, and Wimbledon, as well as the biannual court masques. So Jones and his work were well known to Lord Pembroke who would also have known Isaac de Caux, an "Ingenyear et architecte", who had arrived in England in the 1620s. De Caux was a Huguenot from Normandy, not Gascony as Aubrey thought. He designed grottos in the basement of the Banqueting House in Whitehall, and at Somerset House for Henrietta Maria, both of which came within the purlieus of the Lord Chamberlain. He also designed a grotto in the gatehouse of Skipton Castle, Yorkshire, for Lord Pembroke's second wife, Lady Anne Clifford. De Caux worked for Lord Pembroke at Ramsbury Manor, Wiltshire, a subsidiary house of the Herberts that had been obtained by the 1st Earl after the execution of the Duke of Somerset in 1552. (It was sold in 1676, and nothing now survives of de Caux's work there.) As part of the Jonesian circle of designers known to Lord Pembroke, de Caux was therefore an obvious choice as executant architect at Wilton in the 1630s, especially as he was a specialist in the contrivance of water features and grottos, and the new south garden was a major feature of the 4th Earl's Wilton project.

The original design for the south front was twice the width of the executed building but was curtailed early on. The reasons were political and financial and related to the death of Lord Pembroke's eldest son Charles in 1635 aged sixteen. The dowry of Charles's recently betrothed wife had to be repaid. The match had been recorded in the large Van Dyck "Family Piece" of Lord Pembroke, his wife and children, including the betrothed couple, intended for the Double Cube Room, and one of the great dynastic statements. The curtailment of the Grand Design for Wilton was as much the result of the death of his eldest son and heir, as of any financial retrenchment, for the 4th Earl of Pembroke was still a rich man with his extensive estates, court offices and sinecures.

The garden, however, had been initiated to the scale of the Grand Design, twice the width of the completed south front. Accounts show that work on the garden started in 1632–33 when £200 was spent, with the most expenditure for it (£1,292) in 1634–35.[5] The garden was undertaken before construction began on the south front in 1636–37. This stage involved a slight adjustment of the elevation to take account of the reduced width of the south range, making the west tower containing the entrance to the grounds the centrepiece on the axis of the new parterre. The slight "stretching" of the elevation in order to achieve this, with the tower widened and moved three feet westward, was responsible for anomalies and slight asymmetries in the execution, notably in the Double Cube Room where the chimneypiece is not

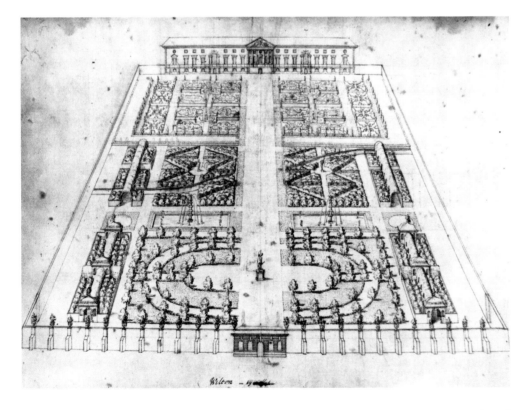

The formal garden looking north, with the Grand Design attributed to Inigo Jones for the wider new front of the house with a regal central portico. The scheme was curtailed after the garden was laid out, only the right-hand section being executed in a modified form from the sketch by Isaac de Caux, as amended by Inigo Jones.

above Marble statues of Flora and Bacchus from the parterre. They are attributed to Nicholas Stone who was paid for carving work at Wilton. Trained in Holland, Stone was the most accomplished English sculptor of the time.

opposite The statues of Flora and Bacchus were resited on the Images Bridge, designed by Sir Richard Westmacott in the early nineteenth century. Several of the sculptures and architectural features from the de Caux garden still adorn the grounds at Wilton.

directly opposite the central Venetian window. These are not immediately discernible to the eye but remain evidence of the change of plan.

The south parterre was the most ambitious formal Italianate garden in the country at that time. The Wilton garden was only the third of its kind to be made in England, Sir John Danvers' smaller Italian pioneer gardens at Chelsea and Lavington coming first. As well as being designed under de Caux's direction, the garden was published by him in *Hortus Pembrochianus* (about 1645) with engraved views of the parterre and the garden structures. Some copies of the book, including the one in the library at Wilton, omit the larger Grand Design for the south front, but some copies do include that engraving, including the one in Trinity College library, Cambridge. The Grand Design was recycled by John Webb for rebuilding Lord Pembroke's London palace at Durham House in the Strand in the 1640s, but that plan was abandoned too, as a result of the Civil War, Durham House meeting the same fate as Charles I's own proposals by Jones and Webb for rebuilding Whitehall Palace.

The team involved in the Wilton garden was the same as that at Somerset House, with both Hubert le Sueur and Nicholas Stone producing sculpture. The Wilton garden paralleled Isaac de Caux's work at Somerset House, and Solomon de Caux's contemporary Elector Palantine's garden at Heidelberg. The Wilton layout was a vast rectangle 400-feet wide and 1,000-feet long, stretching beyond the River Nadder as far as Sir Philip Sidney's walk in the south park. It was divided into three sections with a parterre next to the house bisected by the central walk and divided into twelve rectangular beds with elaborate planting, and four circular pools with marble statues of Venus, Cleopatra, Susannah and Diana by Nicholas Stone. These statues remain at Wilton, having been moved by the 8th Earl to the east forecourt (now in the North Hall). Nicholas Stone (1587–1647) was Master Mason to the crown and had trained as a sculptor in Holland, becoming the key mason-sculptor of the Stuart Court's architectural team.

Moving southwards along the axis there followed a large central area, bisected by the underplayed River Nadder. The axial central path crossed it by a flat bridge. This area was planted as a boscage with small trees and two central ovals on either side containing eight-foot-high giant statues of Flora and Bacchus by Nicholas Stone (moved in 1820 by Richard Westmacott to the park's Images Bridge). Transverse rectangular pools formed elaborate water features with fountains including two rusticated columns with dancing crowns on top. (These columns now flank Westmacott's orangery.) The third and farthest portion of the garden comprised concentric oval lawns and a bronze (described by the seventeenth-century traveller, Celia Fiennes, as "brass") statue of a gladiator facing down the central axis towards the house. (The statue was given to Sir Robert Walpole by the 8th Earl and is now on William Kent's staircase at Houghton.) Flanking both the central and southern sections of the garden were elaborate timber pergolas with open-roofed pavilions and twisted Solomonic columns, the type made fashionable by the Raphael Cartoons for the *Acts of the Apostles* tapestries woven in the new royal tapestry manufactory at Mortlake. These pergolas lasted only about twenty years (the life span of green oak outdoors); by the 1650s and 1660s, they were gone, along with the elaborate parterre planting, and the layout simplified. No doubt this change occurred partly to reduce maintenance during the Civil War and interregnum with its concurrent shrinkage of Lord Pembroke's income.

The *chef d'oeuvre* of the garden was the grotto at the far end of the central walk, with a terrace on top. It contained four large marble panels of classical subjects by Nicholas Stone: two Tritons, Europa and the bull, and Venus rising from the waves (all four moved by Westmacott to the loggia in the west garden, in the early nineteenth century). Stone's involvement in the architectural fabric of the grotto is recorded. The English engraver and antiquary George Vertue (1684–1756) noted that Stone "designed and built many curious works for the Earl of Pembroke at Wilton," and Stone's own notebook records carving work carried out for de Caux.[6] The grotto was admired for its ingenious waterworks and hydraulic tricks, including simulated birdsong and hidden jets to drench onlookers, which were still working, and caught the imagination of Celia Fiennes when she saw the grotto in about 1690.

She described the gardens as very fine with grass squares (which replaced the elaborate flower beds), brass and stone statues, fish ponds and basins. She also admired the flowers and fruit. But her fancy was especially caught by "A Grottoe ... at ye end of the garden just ye middle of ye house – its garnished with many fine figures of ye Goddesses" with "sluce spouts to wet" and a central marble table also with joke jets of water. Hydraulic tricks initiated the "Melody of Nightingerlls and all sorts of birds". She noted that the leaded roof had fish ponds on top, a feature also admired by Lt. Hammond.[7]

The garden was complete by the time of Lt. Hammond's visit in 1636. He was shown round by the 4th Earl's Dutch gardener, Dominick Pile, who was in charge of the planting and management of the place, having been appointed custodian of the garden by the warrant dated 14 March 1635–36. On entering the garden via the undercroft of the south front Hammond records that he met "the fat Dutch Keeper thereof, a rare Artist". He described the garden: "a curious broad Alley of 500 foot long, to a fayre house of Freestone built at the further end of the sayd walke and Garden, below all Archt, ... and pavd with Freestone. The Roofe flatt, and leaded with Freestone Battlements and Water-Pooles; The statues of Venus, Luna, and two more are cut in Marble on the Frontispice; Close to this Banquetting House, is that rare Water-worke now making and contriving by this outlandish Engineer [de Caux], for the Singing and Chirping of Birdes, and other strange rarerities only by that Element, the finishing which rare peece of skill, with satisfaction to the ingenious Artist will cost (they say) a great summe of Money".[8] The waterworks

above left The north elevation Grotto, as depicted in the 1700 painting of Wilton. It was designed by de Caux and echoes the brick and stone treatment of the stables.

above right One of a pair of rusticated Ionic columns from the central section of the de Caux garden. They were originally intended as fountains with dancing gilt crowns supported by spurts of water on top.

top The 4th Earl of Pembroke's Pavilion, originally the bowling green pavilion. The elaborate stone carving is attributed to Nicholas Stone. It was moved in the 1730s and reconstructed again as the schoolhouse in the early nineteenth century.

above left Detail of the carving on the Pavilion, with a Corinthian capital and female bust.

above right The elevation of the Pavilion in its original form from the 1700 painting of Wilton. The redbrick interstices may be artist's licence or could have been replaced in stone by the 9th Earl when he rebuilt it in 1733.

have long disappeared but many of the architectural elements and the sculptures by Nicholas Stone from the de Caux garden survive relocated in and around Wilton.

Another of Nicholas Stone's "curious works" in the garden was the elaborate little pavilion now called the School House, having been moved to a new site to serve that purpose in the early nineteenth century. It was originally the bowling green pavilion overlooking a lawn on the west side of the house, north of the main de Caux parterre. It, the grotto and other garden buildings are shown on a bird's-eye oil painting of Wilton, from about 1700, in the manner of the English country house engravings done by partners Johannes Kip and Leonard Knyff. The painting still hangs in the house.

The Pembroke garden at Wilton had the same theatrical and political dimension as the court masques. It also showed literary influences, with mythical references to Ovid. Beyond the main garden an alley cut through the wood on the opposite hill with a cascade of water and a statue of Pegasus, was an allusion to the springs

above Four carved marble reliefs from the Grotto. Attributed to Nicholas Stone, they depict (*left to right*) two tritons, Venus rising from the sea, and Europa and the bull. They are now incorporated in the Orchid House.

left The interior of the Grotto, from the 1700 painting showing Nicholas Stone's classical marble reliefs on the side walls.

of Helicon. In many ways the Carolean garden was a summation of Wilton as Sir Philip Sidney's Arcadia and succeeded Adrian Gilbert's garden with its elaborate symbolic designs. It, too, had arbours, walks, hedges and fruit trees. John Taylor, who visited in 1623, had described Gilbert as "a true Adamist, continually toyling and tilling ... planting and placing them in such admirable Artlike fashions, resembling both divine and morrall remembrances." Taylor visited Wilton a second time, at the end of the 4th Earl's life, in 1649, after the de Caux reconstruction. He described "the Springs and Fishponds, the Garden, the Walkes, the rare Artificiall Rocks and Fountaines, the Ponds well stocked with fish on the house top, the strange figures and fashions of the water works, the numerous, innumerable varieties of fruits and flowers; yea all and every thing that may make an earthly Paradis, is there to be seene, felt, heard or understood."[9] The garden with its statues and waterworks and above all the grotto was an object of wonder to contemporaries and later seventeenth-century visitors.

The garden formed an appropriate foreground to the 4th Earl's reconstructed house. The south front of Wilton House, as built to the design of de Caux and Inigo Jones, and completed by 1642, was 194-feet wide (as opposed to the 354-feet of the Grand Design). The compact, executed scheme forms a more satisfactory composition than the more expansive Grand Design would have done. The corner

towers provide just the right degree of emphasis for the width of the building, and the carved classical figures and cartouche of the Pembroke arms over the Serliana add enough liveliness to provide a rich centrepiece, contrasting with the plain ashlar stonework on either side. This façade has always been rightly admired as the archetypal English Palladian masterpiece. It is not quite as first completed in 1642. The towers were originally finished with pointed, tiled caps. The present, more original arrangement of pedimented roofs was substituted after a fire in 1646–47 that gutted the interior. The original appearance of the towers is shown in a prefire drawing probably by the topographical artist Wenceslaus Hollar.[10] The towers served a practical purpose as well as providing architectural emphasis. As at Elizabethan Longleat or Hardwick, they served as rooftop banqueting houses or belvederes, with doors giving access onto the lead flats and their excellent views of the garden and park. The Hollar sketch also shows the Tudor outer gatehouse to the east still standing in the 1640s after the south front had been rebuilt.

The conflagration that led to the alterations and refinements of 1647 was caused, Aubrey tells us, by drying the plaster of the new rooms. Although the fire gutted the newly built wing, its outer walls survived. Today, above the restored ceilings of the Single and Double Cube Rooms (originally the Withdrawing Room and the "King's Great Room" or Dining Room) signs of the scorching can be seen on the brickwork, as well as charred ends of timber in the walls and splashes of molten

The South Front by Isaac de Caux and Inigo Jones. It is suggested that the subtle delineation of the corner towers with applied quoins and the breaking forward of the cornice are refinements by Jones. The addition of the flanking tower pavilions *al Italiano* to the de Caux "plot" transformed the design.

lead. The ceilings and roofs of the 1630s range were all destroyed, as were the fittings in the rooms below. The evidence from the structural investigation of 1988–92 also suggests that the present design of the big rooms with high, coved ceilings dates from after the fire and that before, in their first state, these rooms were two storeyed with an upper tier of windows on both sides and flat ceilings, like the Banqueting House at Whitehall. The major elements of the plan – the room divisions and the position of fireplaces, doorways and windows – survived the fire.

On the first floor was a central great chamber, the Double Cube Room behind the serliana, the Single Cube to the west, along with the Hunting Room in the corner tower, on axis with the garden and the king's apartment of anteroom, bedchamber, cabinet or dressing room, and small closet to the east. There was also a cantilevered stone "Geometric" Staircase leading down to the courtyard and up to bedrooms in the south-east corner, immediately to the east of the Double Cube Room where it served as a private entrance to the king's rooms.

The work after the fire included remodelling the tops of the towers with king post roofs, reroofing the building in between with lead flats, and redesigning and refitting all the principal rooms on the *piano nobile*. Aubrey records that Philip, Earl of Pembroke, in 1648, "re-edified it, by the advice of Inigo Jones; but he being then very old, could not be there in person, but left it to Mr. Webb who married his niece".[11] Then in his seventy-sixth year, Jones relied on Webb, whom he had "brought up in the study of architecture", and trained to be his successor. As rebuilt on the original lines by Jones and Webb between 1647 and 1652, the interior once again comprised a royal state apartment. The principal rooms remain the finest testimony to the character of the lost royal Stuart interiors by Inigo Jones at Greenwich, Somerset House, and Whitehall. The rooms were complete by 1652 when Lodewyck Huygens, a Dutch traveller, was shown around and described the interior as a "novelle bastie à l'Italienne" and saw the new ceilings "tout peint d'une assez bonne main." Webb's drawings are dated 1649 and he was paid for building work in 1650 and 1651, as well as an annual fee of £40 as surveyor of the project.[12]

The accounts show that both London and country workmen were employed, including the master joiner Richard Ryder, who worked with Webb elsewhere and was presumably involved in creating the new richly carved wainscot of the state rooms. Lord Pembroke himself, as has been seen, was resident at Wilton at the time, supervising the reconstruction in person. Similar to the Jones-de Caux debate over the responsibility for the façade, there also has been debate over the shared role of Jones-Webb in the interior after the fire. Most of the surviving drawings are in Webb's hand but have annotations by Jones, including in the Wilton archives, a series for doors, indicating that Jones was consulted and was playing a part in the overall design, at least in its early stages.

The exact dating and the political background are crucial aspects for any consideration of the new rooms. At first sight, it seems extraordinary to have embarked on a royal state apartment to receive Charles I after four years of disastrous Civil War, and in the period leading up to the king's execution in 1649. Neither Charles I nor Lord Pembroke ever saw the finished rooms. Lord Pembroke died in the same year

Grottesco painted decoration in the cove of the Single Cube Room by Edward Pearce, with the Pembroke wyvern crest and earls' coronet, *circa* 1647–49. Pearce's painting reaches an Italian level of sophistication.

Edward Pearce's cove in the Single Cube Room with the Pembroke arms and supporters, a spotted panther and a lion argent. Many of the details in Pearce's painting of the cove are the same as the wall carvings in the state rooms, suggesting that Pearce may have had a hand in the design of the latter, including such fanciful details as the "capitals" in the form of wyverns with outstretched wings, swags of fruit and drapery festoons.

as the king, and the job was finished by his son, Philip 5th Earl, with John Webb as architect. But the project has to be considered in the context of the lull in the political strife, following the Treaty of Uxbridge in 1645, and the possibility of compromise and peace. The Earl of Pembroke urged that it would be reasonable for the king to consent to Parliament's demands. Beginning in 1646 and continuing into summer 1647, there was a pause in hostilities, and reconciliation seemed possible between the king and Parliament, certainly Lord Pembroke hoped so. The completion of the interior of Wilton needs to be seen against the backdrop of those reasonably optimistic eighteen months. It was a period when Inigo Jones, seriously affected by the court chaos, had more time for designing, and also for renewing his researches into Stonehenge; thus he would have been in a position to take an active interest in the restoration of Wilton.

Much depends on the exact date of the fire. It is usually said to have occurred in 1647, but it could have been as early as March 1646. The evidence for the date is found in the churchwarden's accounts of St. Thomas's Church, Salisbury, where payment was made for repairing leather fire buckets damaged during the firefighting at Wilton. The relevant accounts cover the year from March 1646 to March 1647, and there is no reason to assume that the payment did not occur in the earlier part of that period. It makes far more sense to have embarked on such an ambitious, semi-royal project during the period of prospective peace and reconciliation, before the final cataclysm and execution of the king, especially as Lord Pembroke himself was a strong supporter of compromise. He had been sacked as Lord Chamberlain at the outbreak of the Civil War, for not being Royalist enough, and had tried to sit on the fence during the conflict. Lord Clarendon sneered that Pembroke would have sacrificed all the royal family to save Wilton, but his aim was a peaceful reconciliation, with Parliament's demands satisfied and Charles I back on the throne as sovereign. This outcome seemed possible in 1646–47 but was doomed by the intransigence of the king. The restoration of Wilton was a reflection of this respite in the hostilities, and it is one in which Inigo Jones would have been able to be involved, as all royal works in London had come to a halt at the start of the Civil War.

An important role was played in Wilton's interior design by another talented member of the Jones *atelier*, Edward Pearce (1598–1658). Pearce was responsible for painting at least four Wilton ceilings: that over the Geometric Staircase (now lost), the coves of the ceilings in the Double and Single Cube Rooms and that of the Hunting Room (also replaced), as well as its wall panels. The vanished new chapel may also have been by him, where the lost, stained-glass window had parallels with Pearce's contemporary design for a stained-glass window for the Mercers' Company in London. As well as painting, Pearce had a significant role in the general design of the wall decorations and ceilings, especially the Hunting Room which was at first intended to be coved like the Cube Rooms, and the Cabinet; ceiling designs by Pearce exist at the RIBA, and at the Ashmolean Museum, which are related to these proposals. The wall decorations in the Cube Rooms with their use of carved draperies, sunflowers, palm branches, heraldic cartouches, and drops of fruit and flowers owe much to Pearce. It is notable that the wall carvings of the Double Cube Room incorporate similar swags and cartouches to Pearce's *trompe* painting on the ceiling cove, suggesting that he had a hand in both; and the carving and painting form a unity. He had an accomplished command of decorative design, as demonstrated in his prosceniums for the court masques at Whitehall, and his mastery of *trompe* ornament, as demonstrated in his publication in 1647 of twelve etchings for ornamental friezes, which were reissued several times up to 1670.[13]

The Roman *grottesco* painting in the Single Cube has been attributed to Matthew Goodricke on the strength of comparison with work by him in the Queen's House, Greenwich. But the painting was by Pearce, as noted by Aubrey, who wrote that Pearce "did also paint all the *grottesco* painting about the new building".[14] And Goodricke died in 1645, so could not have done any work in the post-1646 phase at Wilton. Edward Pearce was the outstanding English draughtsman employed by Jones at the Office of Works, working with both stage design and interior

decoration. A picture emerges not of a dominant architect, but of a Jonesian design team working together at Wilton in the 1640s: Inigo himself as presiding creative genius; John Webb, as executant architect; and Edward Pearce as artist-decorator – all under the personal direction of Lord Pembroke with his aim to emulate the Luxembourg Palace and to have comparable painted and gilded Franco-Italianate interiors at Wilton. Jones's role in the early stages is shown in his annotations on Webb's drawings, but none exist after 1649 and the king's execution, which destroyed his creative skill and will to live. Webb was paid as surveyor of the new Wilton building from 1649 to 1651.

Edward Pearce Senior was the father of the better-known sculptor Edward, Junior (1635–1695), responsible for the famous bust of Christopher Wren in the Ashmolean Museum. But the elder Pearce was also a talented artist who had trained under Rowland Bucket, the decorator and painter at the Court of James I. He had also worked on the interiors of the Charterhouse, including the chimneypiece in the Great Chamber, and Hatfield House, where the organ survives with Bucket's Italianate grotesque decorations, as well as the *trompe* painted decoration of the chapel. Like his master, Edward Pearce was a member of the Painter-Stainers Company, where he became the warden in 1647. He may also have worked in the studio of Anthony Van Dyck in Blackfriars.[15] Pearce is known to have cooperated regularly with John Webb, notably on the interiors for the Earl of Rutland at Belvoir Castle, in Leicestershire, where he died in 1658. He was responsible for painted decoration in the City churches, lost in the Great Fire. He had worked with Jones and Webb extensively on the interior of Somerset House, as well as the new church at St. Paul's Covent Garden, where he collaborated with Goodricke on the large ceiling "with perspective, Groteske and other ornaments" (destroyed by fire in 1795). In the words of George Vertue, he was "a good History and Landskip painter in the reigns of King Charles I and II. He also drew Architecture, Perspective, etc. and was much esteem'd in his time". Gordon Higgott has shown that at least five designs for decoration attributed to Jones were in fact by Pearce.[16] He was influenced by the contemporary French artist and designer Jean Cotelle (1607–76), who published an influential and popular book of engravings of designs for ceilings, *Livre de divers ornemens pour plafonds, centres surbissez, galleries et autres* (1640). Several of the ceiling designs by Webb and Pearce for Wilton in the Worcester College and RIBA collections are based on Cotelle's engravings.

The major Cotelle-inspired room at Wilton is the Hunting Room in the corner tower at the west end of the south range. It was originally called the "Passage Room", or "anti-room" and was designed and painted by Pearce. The walls are lined with eighteen panels of hunting scenes, his best-known surviving work. The subjects were chosen as appropriate for a room on the central axis of the de Caux parterre that led by way of a grand stone staircase to the garden, park and surrounding forests, the royal hunting grounds. The room's decoration reflected Lord Pembroke's enthusiasm for "all sorts of hounds … the stagge … harriers …" The staircase to the garden and beyond was removed by the 9th Earl when he naturalized the garden in the 1730s.

opposite The wall treatment in the Hunting Room by Edward Pearce. The wainscot is inset with his painted panels of hunting scenes. They are based on the engravings of the Florentine artist Antonio Tempesta, published in 1598, which were a popular source throughout seventeenth-century Europe.

following pages The Hunting Room, originally the entrance from the state rooms to the garden and now the billiard room. Double doors lead to the Single Cube Room. The wall treatment with the pronounced dado supported on console brackets is the earliest of its kind in English architecture.

Panel showing bullbaiting in the Hunting Room, one of eighteen panels painted by Edward Pearce. They include English sports as well as more exotic scenes with lions, crocodiles, elephants, ostriches and monkeys derived ultimately from Roman mosaics of gladiator sports.

Pearce's eighteen painted panels in the Hunting Room are arranged in two tiers above and below a high dado with console brackets, the earliest such treatment in English architecture, and a novel design in 1647–49. The panels are separated by pilasters with drapery and cartouches with heraldic wyvern wings derived from the Pembroke crest and a leitmotif of the decoration in the state rooms. The room was enlarged by James Wyatt in 1803, taking in the space of a small staircase to the north, but so carefully done that it does not disturb the seventeenth-century design.[17]

Aubrey describes it: "The anti-roome to the great roome of state is the first roome as you come up staires from the garden, and the great panels of wainscot are painted with the huntings of Tempesta by that excellent master in landskip Mr. Edmund Piers".[18] When first proposed, the ceiling was to be coved, as with the Cabinet Room at the east end, but ultimately both were given flat ceilings in 1649. Pearce's unexecuted design for the cove of the Hunting Room has *trompe* pilaster-panels with cartouches at their top, pendant festoons, and draperies as in the panels below. In this design, as in the Single Cube Room, Pearce intended a unity between the *trompe* ceiling and the wall decoration, again suggesting he was responsible for the design of both, and giving further weight to his leading role in the decoration of the new state apartment. Pearce was involved in the design of the interiors as a whole, not just in executing the decorative painting.

The painted panels are based on the engravings by Antonio Tempesta, published in 1598, except for one of a hare hunt. They are not copies but adaptations, as comparison with the engraved originals indicates. In the execution they were given

Arcadian English landscape settings and all female figures were excluded. They fall into two categories: "English" – hawking, stalking, netting birds, stags, foxes, boar, bulls; and exotic – lions, crocodiles, "wild cats", elephants, ostriches and monkeys, which owed their distant inspiration to Roman mosaics and sculpture. The Tempesta engravings are derived from the artist's etchings in "Primo libro di caccie Varie". Comparison with them shows the inventive way in which Pearce reinterpreted the subjects, transforming his designs to fit square and tall rectangular panels, omitting the side action and concentrating on the main subject against new backgrounds.[19]

The panels were much admired by seventeenth-century visitors and mentioned in the same breath as the Cube Rooms with their paintings by Van Dyck and Emmanuel de Critz (son of the Sergeant Painter to James I). In 1654, when the house was nearly finished, the writer and gardener John Evelyn was impressed by the decoration in

Panel in the dado of the Single Cube Room with scenes from Sir Philip Sidney's *Arcadia*, painted by the Court artist Emmanuel de Critz, one of a series of twenty-six. The inclusion of paintings in the architecture echoed Lord Pembroke's memories of Marie de Medici's Luxembourg Palace in Paris, where he had stayed in 1626, which pioneered the fashion for integrated art in decorating in northern Europe.

"some other apartments as that of Hunting Landskips by Pierce [sic]". Almost four decades later, Celia Fiennes also was especially taken: "Another room is painted with all sorts of sports Hunting, Hawking etc they are all finely painted on the ceiling and very lofty", suggesting that the flat ceiling, substituted for the original coved idea, was also painted by Pearce.[20]

As a passage room, the Hunting Room did not originally have a chimneypiece, whereas in the two Cube Rooms and the king's apartment with its state bedroom and dressing room (also called the "Cabinet Room" because of the smaller paintings that hung there), the four large marble chimneypieces were the dominant architectural feature. These designs formed two tiers with the fireplaces carved in marble, and large classical overmantels of carved wood, pilasters, columns, pediments and sculpture. The chimneypieces are the designs of Jones and Webb, influenced by engravings of the French architect Jean Barbet,[21] and are closely related to Jones's designs for chimneypieces at Oatlands, the Queen's House, Greenwich, and other royal palaces.

The Withdrawing Room, now Single Cube Room, is a striking example of the integration of paintings into the decoration of rooms, as remembered by Lord Pembroke from the Luxembourg Palace. The dado has inset oil paintings of poetic scenes from Sir Philip Sidney's *Arcadia* (written in the 1570s and 1580s and published by his sister Mary, Countess of Pembroke, in 1593) and which was of course written at Wilton. These panels were by Emmanuel de Critz, with whom Pearce had worked at the Queen's House. The coved ceiling is in the Italian grotesque tradition, and was painted by Pearce. It shares many motifs with his 1640s etchings; the stepped groups of panels containing mask heads and drapery swags with scalloped fringes, and sprouting foliage and flowers. Bay leaf festoons link the central compartments of each cove to form continuous border decoration. The festoons of leaves and flowers resemble those of a Pearce drawing in the Ashmolean Museum. Other details are also characteristic of Pearce, such as the oval *trompe* nail fixings, the gilded rosettes and the drapery drops. These, too, demonstrate how Pearce was involved in the design of the room decoration as a whole, and the drapery and rosettes are repeated in the carved and gilded wall treatment. The current gilding in the state rooms dates from the 1820s, but it is clear from seventeenth- and eighteenth-century descriptions that the decoration at Wilton was always heavily gilded, and the white and gold treatment goes back to the original concept, though now more redolent of the lavish luxury of George IV's reign.

The same combination of Pearce and de Critz was responsible for the ceiling of the "King's Great Room", the Double Cube Room. The room's panels by de Critz are oil on canvas and depict events in the life of the mythical Greek hero Perseus, son of Zeus and Danaë, who beheaded Medusa – a suitable subject for a state room planned to receive Charles I. The paintings follow the techniques of Paolo Veronese which Peter Paul Rubens had been inspired by in his spectacular ceiling paintings of 1630–34 for Inigo Jones's newly designed Banqueting House in Whitehall. Like the Rubens' canvases, the panels at Wilton are arranged in enriched compartments – an oval flanked by rectangles – following the similar arrangement at the Banqueting

The ceiling of the Single Cube Room. Edward Pearce's *grottesco* cove decoration surrounds a central panel of the Fall of Icarus on canvas, attributed to the Mannerist artist Giuseppe Cesari, which is said to have been brought from Florence by Sir Charles Cotterell, the English Minister there.

above The Single Cube Room, the withdrawing room of the state apartment. It was created by John Webb and Inigo Jones with the assistance of Edward Pearce. The distinctive chimneypiece was inspired by the French architect Jean Barbet's designs for altarpieces and established a prototype for the Anglo-Palladian interior in the eighteenth century.

above right The east wall of the Single Cube Room with carved pine wainscot painted white and gold, enlivened with Edward Pearce–designed console brackets and drapery festoons.

right Detail of the frieze in the Single Cube Room. The coroneted cartouche with "PM" monogram, for Pembroke and Montgomery, is flanked by the panther, with flames in his ears and mouth, and lion rampant, the supporters of the Pembroke arms, issuing from scrollwork. The palm branches are symbols of fertility and hospitality. The carved swags of fruit echo the painted ones by Pearce in the cove above.

following pages The great doorcase in the
Double Cube Room, open and closed. The
large heraldic cartouche of the quartered
Pembroke arms is topped by the Herbert
wyverns. The frieze also incorporates the
wyvern crest amidst scrollwork. Heraldry
plays an integrated role throughout the
decoration of the rooms, showing Lord
Pembroke's personal input into the design.

House. In the central oval, de Critz shows the unusual subject of Perseus in the palace of the tyrant, King Polydectes, rescuing his mother, Danaë, from the king's unwelcome advances. The scene is set in a grandiose *trompe* interior with Corinthian columns, coffered dome and an open oculus like the Pantheon in Rome. It is possible that this background was designed by Inigo Jones. The rectangular panels show, at the east, Perseus holding the head of Medusa and the winged horse Pegasus that sprang from it; at the west Perseus rides Pegasus and rescues Andromeda from a sea monster. The references to Pegasus echoed the statue situated in the park, beyond the garden, outside the window. The vast coves by Pearce form an appropriately theatrical accompaniment of large-scale swags of fruit executed in a golden brown glow.

opposite The Double Cube Room, looking west with Van Dyck's Great Family Piece dominating the room, and full-length family portraits by Van Dyck filling the rectangular wall panels, reminiscent of Marie de Medici's gallery at the Luxembourg Palace, which was decorated with large canvases by Rubens. The shield of arms on the cloth of estate in the Van Dyck echoes that over the door opposite.

left Attributed to Sebastiano del Piombo, portrait of a shepherd with pipe. This was one of eight Italian paintings given to the 5th Earl of Pembroke by the Grand Duke of Tuscany, Cosimo di Medici, on the occasion of his visit to Wilton in 1669. Five of them remain in the house today.

following pages Emmanuel de Critz, Painting of the mythical Greek hero Perseus in the Palace of the tyrant King Polydectes, rescuing his mother, Danaë. The trompe architecture with Pantheon dome is attributed to Inigo Jones. The ceiling with paintings on canvas framed in elaborately decorated beams repeats that by Rubens in Inigo Jones's Banqueting House, Whitehall.

The dominant element of the integral painted decoration is the series of Van Dyck portraits in the wall panels, including six that are full length and the huge dynastic painting on the west wall, of the Herbert family on parade before a heraldic cloth of estate. These works were all painted in Van Dyck's studio in Blackfriars and brought from London in around 1660 by the 5th Earl (the exact date of their transferral is not known). The placing of the doors and the shape of the panels indicate that the walls were designed to receive them, another indication of the influence of the Luxembourg Palace, where the gallery was designed for Marie de Medici to display the large panels by Rubens now in the Louvre. The whole *mis-en-scène* is transcendently noble, as Lord Pembroke intended.

The state rooms were completed by the 5th Earl after the death of his father in 1649. Although Charles I never had a chance to stay in them, the rooms did serve their royal function for the first time in 1669, after the Restoration, when Cosimo di Medici, Grand Duke of Tuscany, visited the 5th Earl at Wilton, presenting his host with eight paintings from the Medici collection in Florence, five of which remain at Wilton today. He dined in the Double Cube Room in state and spent the afternoon looking at the garden and grotto.[22]

previous pages The Double Cube Room, or King's Great Room, created by John Webb, Inigo Jones and Edward Pearce under Lord Pembroke's personal direction, hung with large portraits by Anthony Van Dyck, is a masterpiece of Stuart royal architecture, and the finest surviving interior of Charles I's Court.

right The marble chimneypiece in the Double Cube Room. The four classical two-tier chimneypieces in the Single and Double Cube Rooms, the King's Bedroom and King's Dressing Room paralleled those by Inigo Jones in the vanished Stuart royal palaces at Whitehall, Somerset House and Oatlands, as well as the Queen's House, Greenwich.

opposite The cove painted by Edward Pearce in the Double Cube Room. More than twelve feet deep, the vast coves are embellished with heraldic cartouches, urns, putti and trompe swags of fruit similar to those of carved and gilded wood trophies, in between the Van Dyck portraits on the walls below. The theatrical character of the gold-hued *grottesco* recalls that Pearce was responsible for the prosceniums and scenery for the Inigo Jones court masques that were performed twice a year in Whitehall for the king and queen.

Anthony Van Dyck, The Great Family Piece of the 4th Earl of Pembroke. The largest and grandest of Van Dyck's English portrait paintings, and one of the most notable European seventeenth-century portraits.

The King's Dressing Room (now called the Corner Room).
The chimneypiece with Corinthian pilasters and pediment,
and marble fireplace surrounded with carved caryatids, is the
fourth of the series in the state apartments. The room was
always intended to be hung with paintings and was described
as "the Cabinet" for that reason by Inigo Jones.

The 4th Earl's rebuilding of Wilton was confined mainly to the south front containing the great rooms. Otherwise he retained his grandfather's Tudor house, including the courtyard with the Holbein Porch that Inigo Jones admired, the north range containing the Great Hall, the East Gatehouse Tower and forecourt with the entrance, though he may have partly regularized the east front to match the new south front. On the west side he divided the gallery into a sequence of two or three anterooms or guard chamber and presence chamber, as an overture to the Withdrawing Room (now Single Cube Room) and the King's Great Room or dining room (now the Double Cube Room) in the new south range. He also built a new projecting chapel near the south end of the west range. A design for this with a prominent window was made by de Caux, based on Inigo Jones's Queen's Chapel at St. James's. This design was not built as shown, but a new chapel was erected there and is shown as a gabled, or pedimented, projection in the Wenceslaus Hollar sketch of the south front before the fire, and other seventeenth-century views. It had a large stained-glass window at the west (liturgically east) end and a tribune or family gallery on the *piano nobile* at the opposite end, the household sitting on the ground floor below. This new chapel was made necessary by the demolition of the 1st Earl's predecessor chapel to make way for the rebuilding of the south range. The 4th Earl's chapel no longer exists. The rooms in the west and north wings were remodelled by successive earls in the eighteenth century.

The King's Bedroom or Colonnade Room is dominated by the third of the magnificent two-tier chimneypieces, invented by Jones and Webb out of ideas for French altarpieces. The cartouche of the Pembroke arms clutched in the "jaws" of the broken pediment, and the marble wyverns holding drapery in the frieze over the fireplace, continue the ubiquitous heraldic decoration throughout the rooms. The absence of the Royal Arms in the state bedroom is indicative of Lord Pembroke's ambivalence toward the king during the Civil War, and contrasts with the ubiquity of royal arms in the Tudor house.

Wilton in its eighteenth-century landscaped setting. The enclosed
Isaac de Caux formal parterre was replaced in the 1730s and 1740s by
the 9th Architect Earl of Pembroke with a naturalistic layout of lawns,
meandering river, cedars and carefully placed architectural features of
which the Palladian Bridge in the foreground is the most significant.
The Wilton park was an early example of the English eighteenth-
century landscape garden and remains one of the most beautiful.

Chapter Three
Art, Sculpture, and the "Wilton Myth"

WILTON AS IT APPEARS TODAY OWES MORE THAN IS IMMEDIATELY OBVIOUS TO
Thomas, the 8th Earl of Pembroke (1656–1733), and Henry, the 9th Earl of Pembroke
(1689–1750), in the first half of the eighteenth century. The former was responsible
for the collections, especially the paintings and antique sculpture, reconstructing
the north wing, and making the house a public showplace, not to mention initiating
the "Wilton Myth", which has proved so persistent for three centuries now. The 9th
Earl, known as the "Architect" Earl, was an accomplished amateur architect whose
taste and abilities as a designer were greatly admired by contemporaries. He was
responsible for the landscape setting with the lawns, cedars and Palladian Bridge,
and he carried out extensive alterations to the house, sashing the windows, embellishing the state rooms and contriving new rooms on the ground floor in the spirit of
Inigo Jones, some of which survive, and generally making the place into a Palladian
dream.

Horace Walpole wrote of the 9th Earl: "The towers, the chambers, the scenes
which Holbein, Jones and Vandyke had decorated, and which Earl Thomas had
enriched with the spoils of the best ages, received the last touches of beauty from
Earl Henry's hand. He removed all that obstructed the views to or from his palace,
and threw Palladio's theatric bridge across the river ... No one had a purer taste in
building than Earl Henry, of which he gave a few specimens besides his work at
Wilton".[1] Walpole added that the 10th Earl, the architect's son, also Henry, "has
crowned the summit of the hill [opposite the house on the south side of the park]
with a statue of Marcus Aurelius and a handsome arch by Sir William Chambers".
This is now moved and forms the entrance to the North Forecourt, as will be seen.

Henry, the 9th Earl of Pembroke, as Walpole makes clear, acted as an architect in
his own right. He inherited his father's love of the arts, which he expressed especially
through architecture. He introduced his father to his friends Sir Andrew Fountaine

Portraits of the 8th, 9th and 10th Earls of Pembroke, all of whom made significant contributions to Wilton in the course of the eighteenth century, embellishing the architecture and creating the art collection that fills the rooms.

above left Willem Wissing. Thomas, 8th Earl of Pembroke (1656–1733).

above right Henry Hoare of Bath. Henry, 9th Earl of Pembroke (1693–1750), the "Architect Earl."

right Joshua Reynolds. Henry, 10th Earl of Pembroke (1734–1794).

(1676–1753), the Norfolk landowner, antiquarian and amateur architect, and the Revd. William Stukeley (1687–1765), the antiquarian clergyman. Fountaine became the honorary librarian at Wilton, and Stukeley, with a strong interest in prehistoric monuments, pursued studies of the stone circles at Stonehenge and Avebury in Wiltshire, refuting Inigo Jones's suggestion that Stonehenge was Roman. These two contemporaries of Henry, the 9th Earl, became the sometimes resident historians at Wilton, helping Henry's father Thomas, the 8th Earl, chronicle the house, catalogue the collections and record their patron's notes and views. Stukeley's catalogue of the sculpture was conceived under Lord Pembroke's direction in 1723 and was the basis of the house-steward Richard Cowdry's *Description* first published in 1751 and the subsequent guidebooks by James Kennedy.

Thomas, 8th Earl of Pembroke, succeeded two owners who played little role in the development and embellishment of Wilton. He was the third son of the 5th Earl who had completed the Palladian reconstruction of the south front in 1652 to the design of John Webb. Thomas himself inherited the title, the house and the estate in 1683 at a low ebb in Wilton's and his family's fortunes. His elder brother William, the 6th Earl, had played no role in public life and had died unmarried in 1674, when his half-brother Philip succeeded him as 7th Earl.

This Philip was the black sheep of the family "chiefly known for deeds of drunkenness and manslaughter", according to Aubrey. Accused of murder and blasphemy,

The Palladian Bridge over the River Nadder, designed by the 9th Earl of Pembroke, with the assistance of Roger Morris, and built by the mason John de Val in 1733. Conceived primarily as a garden ornament, the bridge pays homage to Andrea Palladio and it has been suggested may have been inspired by a sketch of Inigo Jones. On the wooded hill in the background can be seen the 10th Earl's Doric Casina designed by Sir William Chambers in 1750.

he was imprisoned twice in the Tower of London, and finally banished to Wilton by Charles II after killing a watchman at Turnham Green, Middlesex. Although Philip had married Henriette de Querouaille, sister of Louise Duchess of Portsmouth, mistress of Charles II, French spy, and ancestress of the Dukes of Richmond, the couple had no children. When Philip died aged thirty, he left behind huge debts, and Thomas, succeeding him, faced the daunting task of restoring the lustre of Wilton and the family's reputation.

Much had already been sold in the late seventeenth century, including Durham Place in London, the earl's grandfather's house, and outlying estates in Wales, and elsewhere in Wiltshire, including Ramsbury, acquired by the 1st Earl in 1552 after the fall of the Lord Protector the Duke of Somerset, and where de Caux had worked for the 4th Earl. Many of the family heirlooms had also been sold, including the sixteenth-century portraits and Mary Sidney's books; more soon followed to clear the debts. The early years of the 8th Earl's reign were taken up sorting out the business of the estate while also tending to his official responsibilities and political career. Thomas occupied an illustrious position in public life throughout the reigns of William and Mary, Queen Anne, and George I. As well as his personal talents, these official posts owed much to his pleasant character and the fact that he was Tory enough, yet not being Jacobite, while supporting the Williamite and Hanoverian Settlements; his position made him attractive to both sides of the political divide, Whigs and Tories, the former the successors to the Parliamentarian constitutionalists, and the latter the royalist traditionalists.

Thomas was Lord Lieutenant of Wiltshire, the royal representative in the county, a post that had been almost hereditary in the Pembroke family since the 1st Earl's time. He was Lord President of the Council on several occasions, chairing government meetings, and 1st Lord of the Admiralty and Lord High Admiral of England, responsible for the navy during the wars with Louis XIV's France. The model of the seventy-gun ship *Old Hampton Court*, presented to him in this role in 1692, remains at Wilton in its original glazed walnut case. He was also an Elder Brother of Trinity House, the body that oversees lighthouses and buoys around the British coastline, and a commissioner of Greenwich Hospital, the magnificent royal asylum for naval pensioners that occupies the site of the Tudor palace at Greenwich. He also served as Viceroy of Ireland, opening the Irish Parliament in 1707, when he took Andrew Fountaine to serve as Gentleman Usher of the Black Rod for Ireland. He was the British plenipotentiary at the Treaty of Ryswick in 1697, which sealed the Anglo-Dutch curtailment of Louis XIV's expansionist ambitions in the Low Countries. Louis recognised William III as King of England in place of James II. Like the first four earls, he was created a Knight of the Garter, the preeminent order of chivalry in England.

The 8th Earl was educated at Christ Church, Oxford, then went on a Grand Tour of France and Italy in 1676–78, where he befriended the philosopher John Locke in Montpelier, and was much struck by Continental collections of sculpture and art, such as the Justiniani Collection in Rome. His role as a patron, collector and *virtuoso* fanned into flames then and became the dominant element of his life.

The Triumphal Arch, with an equestrian statue of Marcus Aurelius, was designed by Sir William Chambers for the 10th Earl of Pembroke, who had met Chambers during his Grand Tour in Rome; it was Chambers's first significant work in stone on his return to England. Originally sited on the hill to the south, the arch was moved by James Wyatt to the new, north forecourt and now forms the main entrance to Wilton House.

LORD CROMWELL   HOLBEIN

Works of art acquired for Wilton in the seventeenth century, and still in the collection.

opposite Hans Holbein, portrait sketch of Lord Abergavenny, given in exchange to the 4th Earl of Pembroke by King Charles I.

above Lucas van Leyden, *Card Players*.

left Hugo van der Goes, *Nativity*.

Engraving of the east front after a drawing by J. M. W. Turner, published in 1825, showing the gothick oriels, clock cupola and north wing (with Lady Pembroke's apartment), all added by the 9th Earl but removed by Wyatt. The side windows of the gatehouse were filled and painted with trompe-l'œil depictions of the 8th Earl's statues by the Flemish artist Jan Van Reysschoot (1702–1772).

Besides Fountaine and Stukeley, he made friends with contemporary collectors and antiquarians and gathered at Wilton a group of scholars who shared his interests, including Carlo Gambarini, from Lucca, Italy, who catalogued Wilton's paintings, and Sir Martin Folkes (1619–1754) of the Royal Society and Master of the Mint, coins being a special interest of the 8th Earl's. He also became a patron of the philosopher John Locke and was a founding member of the Society of Antiquaries, as well as President of the Royal Society, England's first learned society, established by King Charles II. These involvements were signs of his wider interest in the "sciences". Stukeley, Folkes and Fountaine were fellow members of both groups and were also Freemasons.

Thomas the 8th Earl's principal legacy at Wilton is his collection of classical sculpture and Old Master paintings, "the spoils of the best ages" referred to by Walpole. The earl's aim was to repair the ravages caused by his brother; his main phase of collecting was after 1700, when he was less busy in the public arena, and had time to devote to his scholarly and artistic interests and tastes, and to large-scale collecting and selected architectural improvements. Only traces of the latter now survive, notably the pedimented tops of the flanking towers on the North Front, which had retained pyramidal caps like those shown by Hollar on the South Front, until the early eighteenth century.

The north wing containing the Tudor Great Hall was gutted by fire in 1705, though the stone shell of medieval masonry survived, including an arch that can still be seen in an upstairs corridor above the dining room today, and the courtyard elevation with the Holbein Porch. The 8th Earl rebuilt the north wing internally in the Palladian style with a semicircular vestibule leading off the porch into a two-storeyed rectangular hall with a surrounding gallery, modelled after the one in the Queen's House, Greenwich. He also built a new, spacious, open-well timber staircase called the Brown Staircase at the west end leading to the enfilade of show rooms on the *piano nobile* of the west front and the state rooms in the south front. The plan of the arrangement is shown in *Vitruvius Britannicus* in 1719. The architect of the handsome new interiors within the restored north front is not known for certain, but it has been suggested that it was John James (1672–1746) of Greenwich who was working contemporaneously on the old church at Wilton.[2] As a surveyor and architect he was "eminently competent and trustworthy", though his designs were generally somewhat stolid and lacking in imagination. In 1711, he sent to the Earl of Harley a long list of "Persons of Quality" who could vouch for his character and ability and whom he had "served in the business of their buildings". These people included the Earl of Pembroke.[3] John James is known to have admired Inigo Jones, and living himself in Crooms Hill, Greenwich, he knew the Queen's House well. It is likely that the reconstructed Great Hall at Wilton was based on that at the Queen's House, with a similar balustraded gallery circling it.

The semicircular vestibule may have been more original in concept. Such a geometric space was an unusual feature in the early eighteenth century. Like the hall, its appearance was not recorded. The Wilton vestibule was single storeyed. There remain at Wilton, now forming doorcases in the library, a group of well-carved wooden caryatids of unknown provenance, but presumed to have been removed by James Wyatt when he reconstructed the north wing, so it is possible that they once formed part of the decoration in the vestibule. Both the vestibule and the 8th Earl's Great Hall were the setting for the larger items from his celebrated collection of ancient Roman sculpture, notably the statues and busts from the Mazarin

Wilton House, in Wiltshire, the Seat of the Earl of Pembroke.

Engraving of the east front after a drawing by Conrad Martin Metz, published in 1787. The Roman granite column with a statue of Venus stands in front of the gateway, as placed by the 8th Earl of Pembroke. Young cedar trees, grown from seeds brought from Lebanon, are shown dotted around in pots before being planted in the lawns.

[125]

Plan of Wilton House in
the eighteenth century,
showing the internal layout
before Wyatt's alterations,
from the Wilton edition of
Vitruvius Britannicus, 1719. The
library on the west, added
by the 10th Earl to the design
of William Chambers, is
sketched on in ink.

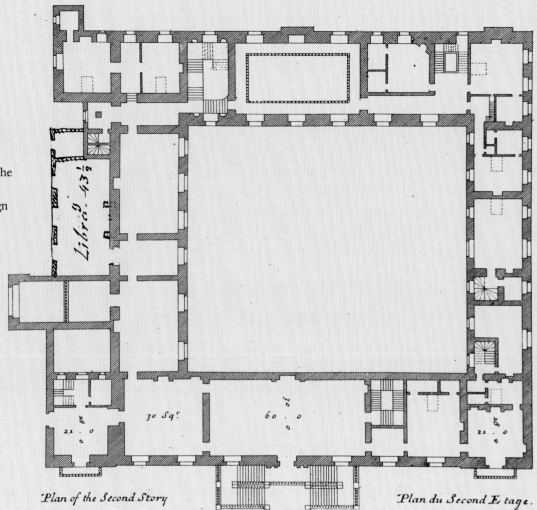

Plan of the Second Story.   Plan du Second Etage.

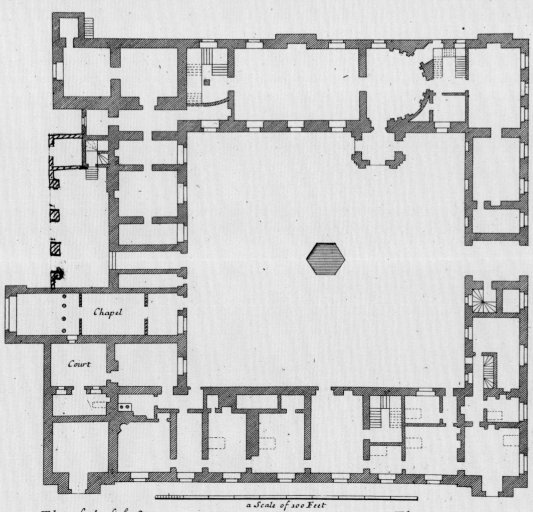

Plan of the first Story.   Plan du premier Etage.

Inigo Iones Inv: A°1640.

Collection in Paris, bought around 1718–20, and the Roman sarcophagi from the Via Appia acquired in 1724.[4] The vestibule contained "two columns of the Pavonazzo or Peacock Marble"; these two tall, fluted Roman columns remain at Wilton and are now in the east Cloister. There were also marble busts on pedestals. The pedestals must have been the set of four handsome "Sicilian Jasper" now in the south Cloister as these have slightly curved backs. Their shape suggests they were made for the semicircular vestibule to match the earlier Roman marble pedestals commissioned by Cardinal Mazarin in the mid-seventeenth century, which were acquired as part of his collection. The Mazarin pedestals continued to support most of the busts as arranged by the 8th Earl at Wilton. The sculpture was very much part of the general architectural effect in the eighteenth-century house.

In the Great Hall were displayed the larger and heavier statues, the marble reliefs inset into the walls, and the sarcophagi. These last were used as bases for statues and busts, to create picturesque, pyramidal compositions in the Italian Renaissance manner, flanking the large marble chimneypiece on the north wall. The display

Roman sculpture collected by the 8th Earl of Pembroke. The Roman sarcophagus is one of five acquired in 1724 from the catacomb of the household of the Empress Livia in the Via Appia, Rome.

Works of art collected by the
8th Earl of Pembroke.

above Raphael, drawing of a cardinal.
A sketch for the frescoes in Julius II's
Raphael Stanza in the Vatican. One of
a number of works acquired by the
8th Earl from the collection of the
artist Sir Peter Lely.

right Jusepe de Ribera, *Democritus, the
Laughing Philosopher* (1636). One of the
most significant Spanish paintings in a
British private collection.

opposite Rembrandt, *Old Woman
Reading.*

Classical busts acquired by the 8th Earl of Pembroke.

below left Bust of Matidia, part Roman, part seventeenth century, from the Mazarin Collection in Paris, bought for Wilton after Cardinal Jules Mazarin's death, *circa* 1718–20.

below right Terracotta of the 8th Earl of Pembroke by Louis-Francois Roubiliac. It shows the earl as a public figure rather than aesthete, wearing armour with the Small George of the Order of the Garter hanging around his neck.

of Roman sculpture continued into the Brown Stairs, where the giant statue of Hercules from the Mazarin Collection was placed in the centre of the well, frightening Cherokee chieftains during their visit to England to meet George III in 1762. The fourth-century AD Triptolemus sarcophagus (depicted in an engraving by Bernard de Montfaucon in *Antiquité Expliqué* in 1719) was placed to one side, supporting the giant bust of Alexander the Great. Apart from the sculpture displays in these new north rooms, the 8th Earl arranged his antique marbles, then the largest collection in England, throughout the state rooms on the first floor, where busts and small statues jostled each other in the west enfilade and the state rooms. George Vertue's drawing[5] of the Double Cube Room shows an array of fourteen Mazarin busts on Roman pedestals, where they remained until the mid-twentieth century, when they were moved to the Cloisters, replacing lesser items which were weeded out and sold after the Second World War.

As well as sculpture in the Great Hall, the 8th Earl placed the 1st Earl's and Henry VIII's suits of armour in niches in the gallery around the first floor. The workaday

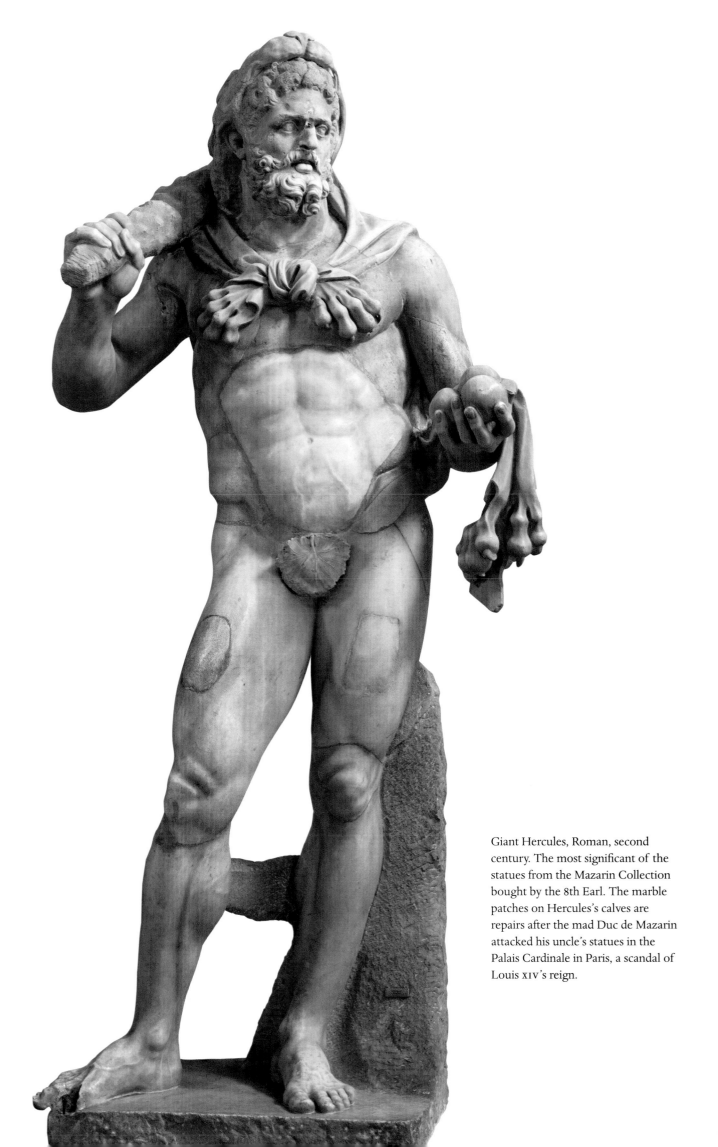

Giant Hercules, Roman, second century. The most significant of the statues from the Mazarin Collection bought by the 8th Earl. The marble patches on Hercules's calves are repairs after the mad Duc de Mazarin attacked his uncle's statues in the Palais Cardinale in Paris, a scandal of Louis XIV's reign.

Works of art collected by
the 8th Earl of Pembroke.

above Peter Paul Rubens, *Christ, St. John
and Two Angels*, detail from the large
canvas in Dresden.

left Andrea da Sesto, *Leda and the Swan*,
based on a cartoon by da Sesto's master,
Leonardo da Vinci. From the Arundel
Collection.

opposite above Pieter Breughel the
Younger, *The Bird Trap* (1565).

opposite below Willem van de Velde,
Seascape. One of three at Wilton.

arms in the Armoury had disappeared during the Civil War, but the splendid sixteenth-century suits of engraved and gilt steel had been retained, and the 8th Earl moved them into the house, where they became a significant prop of the Wilton Myth. Henry VIII's Italian armour worn at the Siege of Boulogne in 1543 was now claimed to be that of Anne de Montmorency, Constable of France "captured by the 1st Earl at the Battle of St. Quentin" in 1557. Similar legendary stories were created for the sculpture, where busts were renamed as emperors, emperor's wives, famous philosophers or poets; illustrious stories were invented for anonymous urns and sarcophagi, which became the "tomb of Horace" and the like, while one innocuous statue became the "father of Julius Caesar when governor of Egypt" and another "the Foster Father of Paris". Much of this invention was Lord Pembroke's, and derived from his studies of Roman medals (coins), and then published in all the successive Georgian guidebooks to Wilton written by Richard Cowdry (1751), James Kennedy (1758) and George Richardson (1774).

The 8th Earl made few alterations to the exterior apart from rebuilding the tops of the north towers after the 1705 fire to match those on the south front with pediments, and the likely demolition of the 1st Earl's outer gatehouse to the east, but he was responsible for minor changes and the display of certain pieces of sculpture in the courtyards, as well as some unusual external decoration. In the inner courtyard, he had the blocked, sixteenth-century mullion and transom windows on the south side painted with *trompe* grisailles of some of the statues in his collection. These windows were later covered over by Wyatt's Cloisters, but a painting of "Cupid wearing a Phrygian cap" came to light during the 1990 restoration and is now visible behind a concealed panel. The same rather eccentric decorative scheme extended to the east side of the gatehouse tower where the side mullion windows were blocked and painted in *trompe* "fresco" by a Flemish artist from Ghent working in England, Jan Van Reysschoot (1702–1772). These paintings made a preview of the sculpture that the visitor was going to see inside the house, like a huge advertising hoarding. These paintings are shown in eighteenth-century engravings.

Not all the sculpture was *trompe*, and a pair of black marble and jasper terms were placed in the sixteenth-century aedicules on either side of the entrance arch in the gate's tower. They are shown in this position in sketches by J. M. W. Turner in 1798[6]. These sculptures were christened the "Viceroys of Persia … out of the ruins of the Palace of Egypt", but were probably sixteenth-century French or Italian rather than ancient Roman. They remain where Lord Pembroke placed them.

The titivation of the gatehouse tower was part of a general improvement of the principal eastern approach to Wilton from Salisbury and London. The forecourt was remodelled along classical lines with an iron *claire-voie*. Beyond, in place of the Tudor gate, towards Salisbury, the River Wylie was canalised with the approach road resited along its south side. In the centre of the east forecourt was placed an Egyptian white granite column said to come from the Arundel Collection, and which had once stood in front of the Temple of Venus Genetrix in Rome, with a copy on top of Giambologna's statue of Venus "brought from Rome by John Evelyn". This story of the column's provenance is another of the Wilton Myths. The column is now in the south-east grounds overlooking the River Nadder. The four statues of Venus, Susannah, Cleopatra and Diana from the de Caux south front parterre were arranged around it by the 8th Earl. To one side of the new forecourt was a pedimented porter's lodge, where eighteenth-century tourists to the house signed the visitors' book. The public opening of the house and its art collections was the initiative of the 8th Earl and continued into the twentieth century. When Celia Fiennes visited in the 1690s, she was told that more than two thousand people had been to the house in that same year. It was to cater for this influx that Lord Pembroke commissioned Carlo Gambarini to write *A Description of the Earl of Pembroke's Pictures at Wilton* (1731), the first art catalogue to be completed of an English country house collection; it was based on Lord Pembroke's notes and information, parallel to Stukeley's catalogue of the Roman sculpture. The *Description* represented Wilton as a repository of one of the world's great art collections, and formed the basis of three subsequent Georgian guidebooks to the house that covered both the sculpture and the paintings. Wilton was a pioneer of the printed country house guidebook. Tourists could buy copies at the house, as well as in London bookshops.

Henry Hoare of Bath. Portrait sketch of Henry, the 10th Earl of Pembroke, as a boy of ten. He wears a jockey's cap, an early indication of his lifelong enthusiasm for horses. He built the Riding School at Wilton, and wrote the horsemanship manual for the British cavalry which remained in use for 150 years.

Henry, who succeeded as 9th Earl of Pembroke on the death of his father in 1733, as we have seen, shared many of the same interests. He, too, was educated at Christ Church, Oxford, where he matriculated in 1705. He subsequently went on the Grand Tour, like his father before him. He visited Venice in 1712, and saw the architecture of Palladio, whom he admired, and spent time in Rome, where he met the eminent English architect, decorator and painter William Kent (1685–1748), and also went to Naples with the philosopher Earl of Shaftesbury. As an undergraduate at Oxford, Henry had come under the influence of Dr. Henry Aldrich (1648–1710), dean of Christ Church, and head of the college, who had encouraged Henry's precocious interest in architecture. Aldrich, a man of wide learning, had a large library of architectural books, and during travels in France and Italy had associated with the "eminent in architecture" on the Continent, according to Walpole; Aldrich, himself a skilled draughtsman, considered Vitruvius and Palladio to be the chief authorities in architecture. Aldrich was much involved in the excellent classical buildings then being erected in Oxford, and he designed the new Peckwater Quadrangle at Christ Church, built between 1707 and 1717, its layout noted for its conscious classicism, which made it a forerunner of the Palladian movement in the 1720s and 1730s. As an undergraduate, Henry subscribed £20 to the building of Aldrich's design for Peckwater Quadrangle, and it is obvious that his enthusiasm for architecture was nurtured during his time at Oxford.

Loggia in the east garden. Originally erected on the dam in the River Nadder, east of the Palladian Bridge, by the 9th Earl of Pembroke. It was resited in the 1820s, when the dam was removed to open up the view east. The "black marble" or touchstone columns come from the interior of the de Caux grotto. On the dam, the arcade was duplicated on either side of the pavilion in the centre.

Apart from work at Wilton, Henry designed for other patrons, including Palladian *villas* at Marble Hill, Twickenham, Wimbledon Lodge, and his own house in White-hall; he also designed the huge Doric Column of Victory at Blenheim and the water tower at Houghton. He also created a summer villa for himself around 1730, Westcombe House, Blackheath, near Greenwich (demolished in 1854). It, too, was a Palladian villa and is recorded in four paintings by George Lambert in the North Hall at Wilton. Lord Pembroke was assisted in his buildings by Roger Morris (1695–1749) who acted as his architectural amanuensis, especially in the work at Wilton. Morris probably came to Lord Pembroke's attention through Colin Campbell, the pioneer Palladian architect and author of *Vitruvius Britannicus* who was a friend of Pembroke's, as architect to the Prince of Wales, and later to George II, to whom Pembroke was the Gentleman of the Bedchamber. Morris had previously acted as an assistant to Campbell. Henry Pembroke valued Morris's services highly, and in 1734 presented him with a large silver cup engraved with a cartouche portrait of Inigo Jones as a token of his regard. The cup bears the inscription: "Given by my Noble Patron Henry, Earl of Pembroke, by whose favour alone I am enabled to fill it. R. Morris 1734".

The principal edifice with which Roger Morris assisted his "Noble Patron" is the Palladian Bridge constructed across the River Nadder to the south-east of the house in 1736–37. It is the chief ornament of the grounds at Wilton which the 9th Earl remodelled to create an early example of the English naturalistic landscape style. In 1740, George Vertue wrote that the bridge was "the design of the present Earl of Pembroke and built by his direction", information that Horace Walpole corroborated.[7] *Vitruvius Britannicus* attributed the design to Roger Morris. This attribution was probably kindness on Lord Pembroke's part: he did not need promotion and publicity, but Morris did. Morris was the executant who supervised the mason John de Val, whose bill for stonework came to £103. The bridge is signed with the mason's initials "J.V. 1737". Lord Pembroke's design was inspired by Palladio's unexecuted concept with a superstructure for Venice's Rialto Bridge, but the Wilton Palladian Bridge is different, and more elegant, and was an original idea that proved influential, forming a prototype that was copied at Stowe, Prior Park and Hagley in England as well as at Tsarskoe Selo for Catherine the Great in Russia. Some scholars have suggested that the design of the Wilton bridge may have been based on a lost sketch by Inigo Jones. The aim was to provide a bridge across the river that also served the visual function of a decorative temple in the landscape, hence the Ionic colonnade and the pedimented pavilions at either end. Seen sideways it is a bridge, but the ends viewed full on appear as temples approached by steps.

The present-day, idyllic classical landscape before the south front at Wilton, with large smooth lawns, majestic cedar trees and the widened river meandering through its midst, replaced the 4th Earl's seventeenth-century formal layout at this time. The work of the 9th Earl was the logical final stage in the gradual simplification of the de Caux formal garden. The elaborate parterres and trellis arbours lasted only one generation. By the 1660s, they had been replaced by grass plots, as shown in a drawing by Count Lorenzo Magalotti at the time of the Grand Duke of Tuscany's

following pages The Roman column acquired by the 8th Earl and originally in the east forecourt, and the 9th Earl's loggia, now overlooking the River Nadder.

visit in 1669, although the de Caux-era statues, axial gravel paths and grotto were still extant.[8] In 1734, the 9th Earl demolished the flanking walls, and grassed over the straight paths, to open up the landscape. He also removed the grotto using its architectural elements on the superstructure of the dam downriver. This new structure was to the east of the Palladian Bridge and built in 1740, but removed in the nineteenth century. The cedar trees may have been introduced by the 4th Earl, and were originally grown from seed in pots, but they were scattered around informally as part of the 9th Earl's programme, while the hill to the south opposite was densely planted as a development of the seventeenth-century wilderness walks to create a wooded backdrop. From the bridge there were views up and down the river, to the east towards the pavilion on the dam and Salisbury Cathedral's spire, three miles away, and to the south-west, the arcaded front of Isaac de Caux's brick and stone classical stables, screening the medieval Washern barn, one of the survivors of Wilton Abbey. The result was one of the earliest Georgian landscape gardens, described by Dr. Waagen from Berlin on his visit to Wilton in the 1840s as "nature converted into paradise"[9].

opposite The Palladian Bridge, seen from the north, was designed by the 9th Earl to read as a temple in the new landscape when seen end on, as well as serving as a bridge.

above The Palladian Bridge, seen from the east, established an architectural prototype which was copied elsewhere in the eighteenth century, notably at Stowe, and at Tsarsko Selo in Russia for Catherine the Great.

following pages The Palladian Bridge, described by Horace Walpole as the 9th Earl's "theatric bridge" thrown across the river.

The cedars at Wilton are a major feature of the garden and are the oldest in England. Over the centuries, as the larger, more ancient trees have succumbed to storms, frost and heavy snow, they have been replaced wherever possible by new trees, from homegrown seedlings, including other tree varieties. Cedars of Lebanon were introduced to England by Dr. Edward Pocock, clergyman to the Turkey Company at Aleppo in the reign of Charles I, who had discovered them growing on Mount Lebanon. He is said to have given cones to his brother, the chaplain at Wilton. Two cedars at Wilton House cut down in 1874 had 236 rings suggesting a planting date of about 1638. The oldest cedars now remaining at Wilton were planted by the 9th Earl from seeds collected in Lebanon by Richard Pocock (of the same family) in 1738. The trees were raised in pots before being planted in the ground, and mid-eighteenth-century engravings show the potted trees dotted around on the lawns.

The Architect Earl's alterations to the main house complemented his work in the grounds. The "touches of beauty" that Walpole admired included the addition of the perfectly scaled statue of Fame with two trumpets, sitting on a globe. She added glamour to the centre of the south parapet, introducing an understated emphasis to the centrepiece that picks up the French-inspired, heraldic ornament of the "Serliana" below, without being overwhelming. Henry was also responsible for some gothick touches on the east front, including a pair of Tudorish oriels intended to keep the gatehouse company, and a lightly gothick north-east wing containing a new apartment for Lady Pembroke, but these were swept away by James Wyatt. Henry's real tennis court to the north, the sport being one of his major enthusiasms, was also removed by Wyatt during his construction of the north forecourt. In the eighteenth century the north side was very much the back of the house, with the

opposite Cedar trees planted on the lawns by the 9th Earl of Pembroke from seeds brought from Lebanon by the Rev. Richard Pocock.

left Lead statue of Victory with two trumpets, added to the centre of the balustrade of the south front by the 9th Earl, one of several "touches of genius".

Anthony Van Dyck, *The Children of Charles I*. Acquired by the 9th Earl and placed by him in the overmantel of the chimneypiece of the Double Cube Room, to complement the royal and family portraits there.

semidetached kitchen block, service wings, tennis court, and other miscellaneous outbuildings and cottages blending into the town.

Inside the house Henry made improvements and embellishments to the state rooms and created new apartments on the ground floor, including family rooms in the east wing, improvements to the show rooms on the ground floor of the south wing, a bathing pool or sunken bath in the ground floor of the south-west tower and another bath in the room next to his bedroom on the east side. Henry was a keen swimmer. When in London, he swam in the Thames in front of Pembroke House, and at Wilton in his new baths; somebody once addressed a letter to him in the River Thames opposite Pembroke House. Altogether Henry was a larger-than-life figure. He was a military man – a lieutenant general – a pugilist, a powerful swimmer and a tennis player. Because of his physical strength he was nicknamed "Samson". He was also a vegetarian, carrying around his leafy dinner in an impromptu bag, made out of an old wig, and nibbling beetroot and watercress as he walked along. His eccentricity was much noted. Horace Walpole described Lord Pembroke's house in Whitehall, designed and built by the earl, as "madly constructed" as himself, and that he was "one of the lucky English madmen who got people to say that whatever extravagance they commit, 'Oh, it is his way'".[10]

For all his attributes, Henry had a terrible temper and could be terrifyingly rude to his neighbours, such as the Duchess of Portland (daughter of Edward Harley,

Earl of Oxford, and a notable collector) to whom he was "scurrilously indecent" in public after she planted trees in front of his London house, blocking the view. People refused to play tennis with him because of his anger and swearing. Despite his irascible side, his rages and his general eccentricity, he also had a deep underlying strain of kindness and generosity, as he showed to his architectural amanuensis Roger Morris in the gift of the silver cup, and also to his wife, Mary, whom he referred to affectionately as "the Rib", referring to Adam's Eve. Mary shared his love of architecture and was called "a great architect herself" by Sarah, Duchess of Marlborough, for whom Henry had designed Wimbledon Lodge and the Victory Column at Blenheim. Thus their improvements at Wilton were a shared enthusiasm of husband and wife.

In the state rooms, the 9th Earl's hand is pervasive, subtly enhancing the Jones-Webb-Pearce architectural decoration. In the Double Cube Room, the earl placed the Van Dyck portrait of Charles I's children in the overmantel framed with carved and gilt drapery and topped with the Prince of Wales feathers, which makes a perfect complement to the flanking seventeenth-century statues of Ceres and Bacchus, gods of hospitality appropriate for the "King's Great Room" used as the dining room. The adoption of names for the state rooms was also the 9th Earl's initiative in the 1730s, referring to their proportions or architectural features. Thus the Passage Room became the "Hunting Room" after its paintings; the Withdrawing Room became the "Single Cube Room" derived from its proportions: thirty-feet square and high. The Great Room or Dining Room became the "Double Cube", thirty-feet wide and sixty-feet long. The King's Bedroom became

The King's Bedroom (Colonnade Room), enlarged by the 9th Earl by removing the back wall and two small closets, and substituting a screen of four Ionic columns to great architectural effect. The beautifully proportioned, fluted Ionic columns frame the bed alcove. Lord Pembroke designed them with his architectural amanuensis, Roger Morris, to whom he gave a silver cup engraved with a portrait of Inigo Jones, as a thank-you for his assistance.

The King's Bedroom.
The seventeenth-century
chimneypiece is adorned with
a painting of the Madonna by
Sassoferrato, encircled by a
garland of symbolic flowers by the
Roman artist Mario Nuzzi. It was
one of the acquisitions of the 8th
Earl, who bought paintings in Italy
with the advice of his honorary
librarian, Sir Andrew Fountaine,
a university contemporary and
friend of the 9th Earl's.

above Andien de Clermont, painting of Roman trophies on the ceiling of the King's Dressing Room, commissioned by the 9th Earl of Pembroke in the 1730s.

above right Luca Giordano, *Conversion of St. Paul.* One of the pictures collected by the 8th Earl, and placed in the centre of the ceiling of the Dressing Room (Corner Room) by the 9th Earl to bring the architecture in line with the Cube Rooms. The framing beam has identical guilloche mouldings to the soffits of the Palladian Bridge designed by him.

right Andien de Clermont, singeries on the ceiling of the King's Bedroom. This *chef d'oeuvre* of English rococo decoration was one of four schemes commissioned by the 9th Earl from Clermont. (Those on the Geometric Stair and in the pavilion on the dam were lost in the early nineteenth-century's remodellings.)

the "Colonnade Room", named after the four fluted Ionic columns introduced by the earl to frame the bed alcove, replacing two small, rear closets. The King's Dressing Room or Cabinet became the "Corner Room" because of its situation in the south-east tower. These new descriptions were cemented by their use in succeeding editions of the Wilton guidebooks, and have been used ever since.

The 9th Earl's only structural change to the state rooms was the enlargement of the bedroom by removing the two small inner closets to the north and substituting the excellently proportioned Ionic colonnade. As with the Palladian Bridge, also with Ionic columns, he was assisted by Roger Morris. He also decorated the ceiling, as well as that in the adjoining Dressing Room, commissioning the French artist Andien de Clermont to paint the ceilings. The bedroom ceiling has charming rococo *singeries*, or arabesques with monkeys, birds and flowers. Clermont lived in England from about 1716 to 1756 after which he went back to France, where he worked in Paris and died there in 1783. He was noted for his flower paintings and his delightful chinoiserie and *Commedia dell 'arte* decorations. As well as painting, Clermont designed tapestries for the Soho Tapestry factory in London and was a leading proponent of English rococo decoration, as patronised by the "Leicester House Set", the artists and patrons around the court of Frederick, Prince of Wales, who was a friend. Lord Pembroke tried unsuccessfully to reconcile that prince with his father, George II.

Clermont's major works included sixteen panels of *Commedia dell 'arte* scenes inspired by the French engravings of Jacques Callot and Jean Bérain the elder for the "Scaramouche" Parlour at Belvedere, Kent, for the 5th Earl of Baltimore (now in the Victoria and Albert Museum); ceilings at Wentworth Castle in Yorkshire and at 5 St. James's Square (the latter now lost) for the 2nd Earl of Strafford; a ceiling at Kirtlington Park, Oxfordshire, for the Dashwoods; and another at Langley Hall, Norfolk, for the Proctors. He was the most avant-garde and inventive rococo decorative artist working in England, and his employment by the 9th Earl is a further demonstration of discerning taste. The Clermont ceiling in the Colonnade Room at Wilton parallels the monkey ceilings in the boudoir at Langley Park, the eponymous temple on Monkey Island in the River Thames near Maidenhead, and a recently discovered example in a house in St. Martin's Lane, near to Leicester Square, in London. Clermont's work at Wilton forms a light-hearted counterpoint to the solemnity of the classical architecture. It has been seen as too slight for its surroundings but is perfect for a bedroom.

Clermont also worked on the ceiling of the Dressing Room, or Corner Room, adjoining the Colonnade Room. There the ceiling painting is more martial in spirit, less lighthearted and composed of *trompe* Roman military trophies in darker colours. This ceiling is unique in Clermont's work and obviously reflects the character of the 9th Earl himself, in his guise as a military man. After Oxford and his Italian Grand Tour the earl entered the army and followed a military career, being promoted to lieutenant general. He became a Lord of the Bedchamber and Groom of the Stole to George II, such household posts often being held by soldiers, and he thus started a continuous family tradition of

The Great Anteroom, chimneypiece and Palladian overmantel glass designed by the 9th Earl for his new ground-floor rooms on the south front, resited by James Wyatt.

military service and membership of the Royal Household that lasted down to the twentieth century.

The ceiling of the Corner Room is entirely the 9th Earl's concept. Inigo Jones and Edward Pearce had produced designs for a coved ceiling with stucco decoration and painted *grotteschi* like the Cube Rooms, but these were not executed in 1649, leaving the room with a flat plaster ceiling. The 9th Earl brought the decoration into line with the bigger state rooms by inserting Luca Giordano's painting *The Conversion of St. Paul* into the centre, framed by stucco "beams" with guilloche moulding identical to those on the ceiling of the Palladian Bridge, and filling the outer margin with Clermont's martial trophies and medallions of Roman victors. Luca Giordano's work was one of the Italian paintings acquired by the 8th Earl and had been hung on a wall until moved to the Corner Room ceiling in the 1730s. The similar placing of the painting of Lorenzo Sabbatini's *The Birth of Venus* in the ceiling of the adjoining Closet was also done by the 9th Earl around 1730, at the same time as the embellishment of the Dressing Room. The painting previously hung in the Single Cube Room.

In addition to his painted decorations on the ceilings in the King's Bedroom and Dressing Room, Clermont was also employed to paint the walls of the Geometric Staircase leading down to the Stone Hall on the ground floor, out of the east end of the Double Cube Room. Clermont's paintings there were destroyed around 1806, when Wyatt removed that staircase and created the Great Anteroom to give access from the Cloisters to the state rooms. Some fragmentary traces on the walls were discovered during investigations at the time of the 1990 restoration of the south range. Clermont's scheme took the form of windows or aedicules decorated with arabesques on a stone-coloured ground. Clermont also decorated the interior of the pavilion on the dam over the River Nadder with "grotesque figures and ornaments".

As well as the work to the state rooms on the *piano nobile*, the 9th Earl also remodelled some rooms on the ground floor to his own design. In the south range he redesigned the central Stone Hall from the courtyard (under the Double Cube), which served as the exit from the show rooms for eighteenth-century tourists, and where further busts and statues were displayed. Another smaller room was created on the ground floor for the sculptural reliefs from his father's sculpture collection. This enabled him to thin out some of the sculpture in the rooms on the *piano nobile*, which tourists complained had more the appearance of a cluttered dealer's shop than a house, and to create more of the effect of a dedicated sculpture room or gallery according to contemporary Georgian taste, as found at Holkham, Farnborough, Petworth and other houses. The ground floor of the Geometric Staircase was embellished by placing in the centre well a life-size statue of Shakespeare, one of the cultural heroes of Wilton, recalling the literary patronage of the 2nd Earl and his wife, Mary Sidney. The sculpture was commissioned from Peter Scheemakers in 1743, and cost about £100.[11] It is a close replica of Scheemakers's other Shakespeare sculpture, made to the design of William Kent, whom Lord Pembroke knew well from Roman days, located in Poets' Corner at Westminster Abbey. One of the differences between the two versions is their inscriptions. On the scroll of the Wilton

The Small Smoking Room, one of the family rooms on the ground floor of the east wing designed by the 9th Earl. It was his, and later his son, the 10th Earl's, bedroom. The present name is mid-Victorian.

statue is a quotation from *Macbeth*, whereas the Abbey's statue has a quote from *The Tempest*. The 9th Earl must have chosen the Wilton lines:

> *Life's but a walking shadow, a poor player,*
> *That struts and frets his hour upon the stage,*
> *And then is heard no more. It is a tale*
> *Told by an idiot, fall of sound and fury,*
> *Signifying nothing.*

The Shakespeare statue is now the centrepiece of Wyatt's North Hall, all the 9th Earl's work on the ground floor of the south wing having been remodelled in the early nineteenth century, though the chimneypieces and pedimented overmantel mirrors were reused in other rooms.

The private family rooms which Henry designed in the east range do survive, now called generically the Smoking Rooms. The suite of rooms comprised Henry's bedroom and a larger rectangular family drawing room on the ground floor. Lady

The Large Smoking Room. The furnishings reflect the 10th Earl of Pembroke. The three bookcases and the writing table in the centre are by Chippendale and were made for the 10th Earl's reconstruction of Pembroke House, Whitehall, to the design of Sir William Chambers. Chambers had a hand in their design. The two smaller bookcases are shown in his design for Lord Pembroke's Room in Whitehall, and the carving on the desk repeats that in the marble chimneypiece there (which survives in an office in the Ministry of Defence).

The Large Smoking Room, designed by the
9th Earl as part of a private apartment in the
east wing. It served as both a dining room and
drawing room in the eighteenth century.

Pembroke's apartment, including winter and summer bedrooms, was on the floor above. The Architect Earl, assisted by Roger Morris, consciously emulated Inigo Jones so successfully that these rooms were soon taken to be the master's work and were treated with reverence by James Wyatt and later generations for that reason. The scroll frieze and cornice, carved door architraves, marble chimneypiece and carved wood overmantel are evidence for Lord Pembroke's mastery of Palladian architecture. Adjoining the ground-floor drawing room (now Large Smoking Room) was the Earl's bedroom (now Small Smoking Room), and his handsome doorcases with carved entablature, a modillion cornice, and a black-and-white marble chimneypiece with Ionic columns survive there, too.

The 9th Earl's interest in architecture was demonstrated on a public scale by his strong promotion and chairmanship of the committee to build a new bridge across the Thames at Westminster, the first over the river since the medieval London Bridge. Against strong vested interest and the criticism of other architects, he supported the Swiss engineer Charles Labelye and the use of the caisson method to build the supporting piers. The first stone was laid in 1739, and the bridge was completed in 1749. However, the whole undertaking and the attacks from disgruntled dissenters so annoyed the earl that he flew into one of his rages and died of a stroke not long after, in 1750. His will shows both his eccentricity and basic kindness of heart; he asked that all his dogs and horses "shall be well taken care of", not worked, and allowed to live out their natural lives in happy retirement in the park at Wilton. He also left money to his mistresses with the proviso that their husbands should not spend it.

His only son, Henry, succeeded to the earldoms and to Wilton. He went to Eton, the first member of the family to go there, leaving in the year his father died, and then went on an extended Grand Tour to Italy and France from 1751 to 1755, which had a profound effect on his artistic interests and patronage. Following his father's death, his mother married Major North Ludlow Bernard (1705–1768), and the 10th Earl became very close to his stepfather, who encouraged his enthusiasm for horses and the military. Major Bernard, of Castle Bernard, County Cork, came from an Anglo-Irish family and was the grandson of General Ludlow. His grandson in turn became Earl of Bandon. He was a distinguished soldier in the Dragoon Guards. He left his library to his stepson, and many books with his bookplate survive in the library at Wilton. From the major, the 10th Earl derived his interest in military horsemanship, which he developed on his Grand Tour when he took riding lessons from Baron Reis d'Eisenberg in Pisa, the master of *haute école* horsemanship and author of *The Art of Riding a Horse or Description of Modern Manège in Its Perfection* (1760). Eisenberg had trained in the Spanish Riding School in Vienna under Monsieur de Regenthal, so Lord Pembroke's training was at the heart of European tradition.

Lord Pembroke commissioned from Eisenberg in 1755 the unique set of fifty-five gouaches depicting horses in different *haute école* positions, which hang in their original red lacquer frames in the Large Smoking Room at Wilton. Lord Pembroke used his training and knowledge to write the standard manual on cavalry movements

Baron Reis d'Eisenberg, from a set of fifty-five gouache paintings of *haute école* horsemanship, commissioned by the 10th Earl on his Grand Tour in 1755. He took riding lessons from Eisenberg in Pisa.

for the British Army, which remained in use for over a hundred years. He used the Wilton estate to train military recruits, building a riding school partly for that purpose to the north-west of the house. He employed an Italian riding master, Domenico Angelo, to teach horsemanship there. During his Grand Tour in the 1750s, he had commissioned the school's design from the French architect Jean-Baptiste Vallin de la Mothe, who at the time was studying at the French Academy in Rome under the Parisian neoclassicist Jacques-François Blondel. In 1759, de la Mothe went on to St. Petersburg, where he designed the Small Hermitage for Catherine the Great's art collection, the Imperial Academy of Arts, several palaces and the Catholic church of St. Catherine.

Lord Pembroke embarked on the riding school's construction the moment he returned to Wilton from his travels in 1755. He used only de la Mothe's design for the visible, ashlar stone-faced south end, facing the garden, with a large blank arch, central pediment and flanking sculptural panels. Otherwise, the riding school was built in brick on simpler lines by the local building team, possibly employing a

Vallin de la Mothe, design for the Riding School at Wilton, commissioned by the 10th Earl during his Grand Tour in 1755, while de la Mothe was studying at the French Academy in Rome. (The architect later went to St. Petersburg to work for Catherine the Great, where he designed the Small Hermitage.)

First ERICHTHONIUS dar'd with dauntlefs Skill
To yoke four Steeds and guide the Victor's Wheel
THESSALIA taught the Conduct of the Bit,
To mount the Steed, and from his pliant Feet,
To paw the Ground, to wheel, to turn with Grace
To tread the Plain with more majestic Pace,
To fly, to ftop, the Rules of War to know,
T'obey the Rider, and to dare the Foe.

When now his Strength and youthful Years decay
With no inglorious Ease his Toils repay,
But grant him, of thy Bounty, still to close
His honor'd Age at Home in soft Repose,
In Peace t'enjoy his former Palms and Pains,
And gratefully be kind to his Remains.

ship's carpenter. The structure is noted for its impressive, wide-span timber roof with complex double trusses incorporating king posts and queen posts in a master-work of carpentry. The homelier English character of the interior is obvious in the timber viewing gallery at the north end, with a "Chinese Chippendale" balustrade and central Venetian window. It retains the painted boards inscribed with Lord Pembroke's own verses celebrating the "Maneged horse":

> First Erichthonius dar'd with dauntless Skill
> To yoke four Steeds and guide the Victor's Wheel
> THESSALIA taught the conduct of the Bit,
> To mount the Steed, and from his pliant Feet,
> To paw the Ground, to wheel, to turn with Grace
> To tread the Plain with more majestic Pace.
> To fly, to stop, the Rules of War to know,
> T'obey the Rider, and to dare the Foe.
> When now his Strength and youthful Years decay
> With no inglorious Ease his Toils repay,

Painted boards in the Wilton Riding School. The verses celebrating the manèged horse were written by the 10th Earl himself. He described himself "being, I fear, as horse mad as my father was tennisly so".

[161]

First ERICHTHONIUS dar'd with dauntlefs Skill
To yoke four Steeds and guide the Victor's Wheel
THESSALIA taught the Conduct of the Bit,
To mount the Steed, and from his pliant Feet,
To paw the Ground, to wheel, to turn with Grace
To tread the Plain with more majestic Pace,
To fly, to ftop, the Rules of War to know,
Tobey the Rider, and to dare the Foe,

When now his Strength and youthful Years decay
With no inglorious Ease his Toils repay,
But grant him, of thy Bounty, still to close
His honor'd Age at Home in soft Repose,
In Peace t'enjoy his former Palms and Pains,
And gratefully be kind to his Remains.

The interior of the 10th Earl's Riding School. It is one of only three Georgian riding schools to survive in England. Lord Pembroke used Vallin de la Mothe's sophisticated neoclassical design for the south facade visible from the garden, but the interior with a wide timber roof and "Chinese Chippendale" viewing gallery is a much more homely English job by local builders.

David Morier, equestrian military painting, one of a set commissioned from the Anglo-Swiss artist, who settled in England in the 1740s, under the patronage of the Duke of Cumberland, for whom he painted a record of the Battle of Culloden.

But grant him of thy Bounty still to close
In Peace t'enjoy his former Palms and Pains,
And gratefully be kind to his Remains.

Lord Pembroke described himself as "being, I fear, as horse mad as my father was tennisly so".[12] Another sign of his horse enthusiasms is the group of paintings he commissioned from David Morier, the Swiss artist patronised by the Duke of Cumberland, for whom he painted a view of the Battle of Culloden in Scotland (1745), and thereafter recorded the regiments and uniforms of the British Army for the duke and other senior officers including the 10th Earl of Pembroke who rose to the rank of general, fighting in the Seven Years War (1756–63), where he commanded a troop of cavalry, and became Colonel of the Royals (one of the regiments of the Household Cavalry). Morier's paintings commissioned by the 10th Earl show cavalry training in the park at Wilton with Lord Pembroke, his son George Lord Herbert (the future 11th Earl) and supporting officers, including Lieutenant John Floyd who accompanied the latter on his Grand Tour to Vienna.

While in Rome the 10th Earl met the artist Richard Wilson (1714–82), from whom he bought Italian landscape paintings, and commissioned the famous series of five views of Wilton upon his return to England. In Rome he also came across Sir William Chambers, the architect who, like de la Mothe, had begun his career in Paris under Blondel before going on to Rome for five years from 1750 to 1755, the same years that the 10th Earl was in Italy. The 10th Earl also met there

above Richard Wilson, *Tomb of the Horatii*, acquired from
the artist in Rome by the 10th Earl on his Grand Tour in
1755.

opposite and following pages Richard Wilson, *Five
Views of Wilton*, commissioned by the 10th Earl on his
return to England, and recording his and his father's
remodelling and embellishment of the park at Wilton
with the Palladian Bridge, pavilion on the dam, and
Chambers's "Casina" and Triumphal Arch, as well as the
spire of Salisbury Cathedral, three miles to the east.

Sir William Chambers, the "Casina", designed for the 10th Earl in Doric style to be an eye-catcher on the hill south of the house and a place for picnics. The ground floor contained a kitchen, and the main room opened into the portico with a view of the south front and the Palladian Bridge in their landscaped setting.

the sculptor Joseph Wilton (1722–1803), and, like Chambers, a future founding member of George III's Royal Academy. In 1760, Wilton carved two copies of the Apollo Belvedere and the Medici Venus for Lord Pembroke to add to his sculpture collection. On Lord Pembroke's return, Chambers was commissioned to design buildings in the park at Wilton in 1759–60, including the "casina",[13] a pedimented, two-storeyed temple eye-catcher on the wooded hill south of the house across the River Nadder, and the triumphal arch supporting an older lead statue of Marcus Aurelius, which is thought to date from the 8th Earl's time. Chambers tells us that the arch was his first work executed in stone upon his return to England from Italy. It was moved to the north forecourt by Wyatt but survives as one of Chambers's most handsome early works. A rockwork bridge across the Nadder constructed to Chambers's design, as well as the model for it, has disappeared.[14] Chambers was also employed subsequently by Lord Pembroke to remodel the west wing, where a new dining room was created, and also a library fitted up in 1761–62 (a library catalogue was compiled in 1773); however, both dining room and library were lost (and unrecorded) when Wyatt demolished that side of the house in the early nineteenth century to create the larger Regency library-living room that continues to serve that purpose today. Until Chambers, that side of the house had comprised an enfilade of three interconnected rooms used to display the 8th Earl's art collections, and to act as anterooms to the seventeenth-century chapel on the west and the state apartment on the south front. As shown in the plan in *Vitruvius Britannicus* in 1719, and described in consecutive editions of the eighteenth-century guidebooks, a passage at the top of the 8th Earl's Brown Stairs led to an enfilade of three rooms: the White Marble Table Room, which was remodelled by Chambers to become the dining room in about 1761–62, and referred to in the ninth edition of the guidebook (1774) as the "New Dining Room", a small central anteroom called the Closet, and the Chapel Room which served as access to the family tribune of the two-storeyed chapel, and to the Single Cube Room and Hunting Room to the south. A new billiard room was made on the ground floor around 1760. The Dining Room contained two mahogany Chinese Chippendale side tables, with red Egyptian granite tops, now in the present-day dining room, while the chimneypiece garniture consisted of three terracotta busts by the Huguenot sculptor Louis-François Roubiliac (1702–1762) with the one of Thomas, the 8th Earl, who "collected all these antiquities" in the middle surveying his pictures and busts. The remodelling of the west rooms involved a rearrangement of the sculpture and paintings there, though the state rooms largely remained as arranged by the 8th and 9th Earls, apart from moving two full-length portraits by Van Dyck from between the windows and their replacement with a pair of large pier glasses, to enhance the light.

The 10th Earl was also responsible for employing William Chambers to extend and reconstruct his father's house at the Privy Gardens at Whitehall, to make one of London's finest Georgian town houses. It was given up by the family in 1827, on the death of the 11th Earl, and was used as government offices in the nineteenth century. It was demolished in 1936 to make way for the Ministry of Defence, but some of its interiors with plasterwork and marble chimneypieces were reconstructed inside its gigantic successor. For the interior, Thomas Chippendale (whose receipts survive in the Wilton archives) was employed to make the furniture in 1764, for which he was paid £1,500. The Chippendale furniture was all moved to Wilton in 1827 including mahogany hall chairs, gilt brass hall lanterns, carved and gilt drawing-room furniture, but above all the library table and three glazed mahogany bookcases from Lord Pembroke's room in the Whitehall house. The pair of smaller bookcases are shown in Chambers's 1760 drawing for the room in the Wilton archives. The larger bookcase carved with a rococo trophy of musical instruments is a masterpiece of English cabinetmaking. The library table has classical carving that repeats that in

Looking glass in the King's Closet (Little Anteroom), one of several similar mirrors, designed by the 9th Earl for the ground-floor rooms on the south front, now resited around the house.

the chimneypiece frieze of Chambers's design for Lord Pembroke's Room at White-hall. All of this furniture set is now reassembled in the Large Smoking Room at Wilton, where it complements the Eisenberg *haute école* horse pictures in the 9th Earl's drawing room as a *renvoi* of Georgian Wilton.

The works of improvement by Chambers and the 10th Earl were completed in time for the visit of George III and Queen Charlotte in 1778, which coincided with a review of troops for the American War of Independence, an event written up by the family chaplain, the Rev. Thomas Eyre.[15] This visitation was important to Lord

Pembroke both in recognising his military role and in demonstrating a public sign of rehabilitation after the scandal of his marriage betrayal, and he made elaborate arrangements for the occasion. Soon after his marriage to Elizabeth, the beautiful daughter of the Duke of Marlborough, the 10th Earl had run off to France with Kitty Hunter, the daughter of an official from the Admiralty Office, resigning all his positions as a general and a Lord of the Bedchamber to George III, and producing an illegitimate son. After a year he had returned to his wife and gradually had been restored to the royal fold, finally receiving the favour of the official royal visit to Wilton. It was the last time the state apartment was used for the purpose it was designed for, with the king sleeping in the King's Bedroom.

There was no bed in the state bedroom, and a magnificent bed was borrowed for the occasion from the Beckfords, neighbours at Fonthill Splendens a few miles to the west. But this bed was not used by the royal couple. As Dr. Thomas Eyre wrote: "Lo and behold, when they arrived they brought a snug double tent bed, had it put up in the colonnade room where the state bed was already placed".[16] There king and queen slept quietly surrounded by the Joshua Reynolds portraits which Lord Pembroke had recently commissioned of his relations and hung there.

Lord and Lady Pembroke greeted the king and queen upon their arrival at the Holbein Porch, the royal carriage having come right into the quadrangle that had been re-gravelled for the occasion. They then accompanied the royal party through the Great Hall, up the Brown Stairs and along the western enfilade, following the tradition for all the royal visitors before them, to the Double Cube Room where George III formally received the mayor and corporation of Wilton who gave speeches and presented a loyal address. The king ate dinner in the "New Dining Room" surrounded by those above the rank of colonel. The queen dined separately with her ladies-in-waiting, Lady Pembroke, Lady Egremont and Lady Weymouth. There were also four other dinners served at the same time: the aides-de-camp in the Corner Room; the Mistress of the Robes, Miss Herbert, the king's secretary and comptroller and Dr. Thomas Eyre the chaplain – all downstairs together; in the Stewards Room, the royal pages and the footmen; and in the Servants Hall, the other servants. After dinner there were cards in the Double Cube Room and conversation in the Single Cube. The queen used the Corner Room as her dressing room, fulfilling its original purpose; it was also used for breakfast the following morning, after which Lord Pembroke showed the royal party around the house, before the king left for the military review. It was the last time that the Wilton state apartment was used for its original purpose, with all the formality of a state occasion, resembling a royal palace. Cultural, social and economic changes would shortly transform English country houses from formal abodes with state apartments to comfortable private houses for family life and more relaxed house parties with a range of informal entertainment. Throughout the country, old houses were remodelled to meet new social expectations in the Regency period. Wilton was no exception.

Chapter Four
Wyatt "The Destroyer"

AS IT EXISTED IN 1800, WILTON WAS A GREAT HOUSE BEREFT OF MODERN comforts. The focus of the building was the famous south front by Inigo Jones and Isaac de Caux, overlooking the park, with its grand but comfortless enfilade of state rooms on the *piano nobile*. There were also one or two Georgian remodelled family rooms within the west and north wings, including the 8th Earl's two-storeyed Palladian or "Grecian" hall, possibly by John James of Greenwich, the 9th Earl's drawing room and bedroom, and a new library and dining room designed by Sir William Chambers for the 10th Earl in the west range, as described previously.

After George Herbert, the 11th Earl, inherited Wilton in 1794, his first priority was to put his finances in order – always a consideration at the beginning of a new "reign" – and then to try to modernise his house. The choice of James Wyatt as architect was obvious: Wyatt was George III's favourite architect, Surveyor General of the Office of Works responsible for royal and government buildings and architect to the Board of Ordnance, and the Pembrokes were close to King George III who had been the last monarch to occupy the Wilton state apartment on the royal visit in 1778. But the decision was also encouraged by Wyatt's contemporaneous work for William Beckford at Fonthill, the neighbouring estate to the west, which promised the practical advantage, sadly not to be fulfilled, of frequent site visits to Wilton by the architect.

Lord Pembroke had a clear idea of what he wanted. The south and east fronts were to be retained, the "Inigo Jones" state rooms treated with absolute respect, and the irregular mix, medieval, Tudor, and Georgian, west and north sides rebuilt to contain modern family rooms. Meanwhile, new corridors were to be added around all four sides of the quadrangle along with a new entrance positioned to face the town to the north. As he told his cousin, the Earl of Caernarvon, of Highclere Castle in Hampshire, in October 1800, the earl wanted "to give a large house the comfort

below The Gothic Stairs seen from the Gothic Hall, a key part of Wyatt's internal replanning. The stairs are his preferred imperial plan, beginning in a single, central flight and returning in two flights. They cleverly serve two levels, the main floor at half landing, and the east wing bedrooms on the upper.

and convenience of a small one". Lord Caernarvon advised him to spend his money on good new, Gothic interiors and to keep the exterior simple in the style of Inigo Jones.[1]

The first proposals in 1801–02 were in fact more economical than the drawn-out final result. Wyatt produced a scheme for creating a semicircular north forecourt on the model of Lord Burlington's at Burlington House in London, reusing the quadrant colonnades of Doric columns from Fonthill Splendens that William Beckford was in the process of demolishing, having decided to make Wyatt's Fonthill Abbey,

opposite The Gothic Hall is the prettiest of Wyatt's new Gothic interiors, with its stucco rib vault by Francis Bernasconi. It fills the open archway in the Tudor gate tower.

originally intended as a park folly, into his main home. Some salvaged material from demolished Splendens was reused at Wilton including masonry and paving but not the colonnades. Wyatt also suggested treating the north front like the east front, with a Tudor centrepiece and flanking "Inigo Jones" links and corner towers. In this case the intention was to reuse the Holbein Porch which was carefully dismantled and its stones numbered to make way for the new Cloisters inserted inside the quadrangle; a plan by Wyatt shows the porch placed centrally to create a symmetrical

new north façade. This idea was not adopted as Lord Pembroke wanted the new front to be Gothic and Wilton partly restored as an "Abbey". Wyatt's idea of moving Sir William Chambers's Arch of Marcus Aurelius from the hill in the park to form the new entrance into the north forecourt was adopted with brilliant effect, and there it makes a splendid overture to the house. But instead of a classical court and façade Wyatt produced a rather weak symmetrical Gothic effort and a long, rectangular forecourt, flanked by crenellated walls with fake windows, none of which found much favour with subsequent generations and led to extensive remodelling in the twentieth century. The Holbein Porch was in the event reconstructed under the direction of the sculptor Sir Richard Westmacott (1775–1856) as a garden feature to the west of the house in 1826. Its careful salvage and reconstruction is evidence of Lord Pembroke's and Wyatt's respect for the "Holbein" and "Inigo Jones" work at Wilton. Westmacott, who had trained in Rome under Antonio Canova, was one of the most successful sculptors in early nineteenth-century Britain. He was Wyatt's friend and protégé, and they often worked together.

Wyatt's easygoing attitude to his client's wishes and his delegation to subordinates are symptomatic of the professional weaknesses that led to defects and uneven quality in some of the architect's later designs. If he had been more single-minded in pushing his own ideas, the buildings might have been better. But his personal charm and malleability were part of his appeal to his architectural clients and patrons. There is no doubt that the early classical version for the north front of Wilton, reusing the Holbein Porch and the crescent-shaped colonnaded forecourt, would have been superior to the scheme that was achieved eventually with great expense and acrimony in 1809–10.

Wyatt's great success at Wilton was in replanning the interior, regularising the floor levels, improving communications and generally working wonders to knit together the piecemeal remodelling of a medieval monastic layout and provide Lord Pembroke with up-to-date accommodation: guest bedrooms, a library–living room, a large formal dining room, and convenient access corridors. Wyatt also showed his progressive approach to the use of modern building materials, using cast-iron sections to strengthen old beams, and adding a new, quick-drying stucco – "Parker's cement" – to the elevations of the Cloisters. The product (from Sheppey in Kent) was manufactured by Wyatt's cousin Charles, and the architect also used the revived stained-glass techniques of his cousin Maria (Wyatt) Eginton of Birmingham.

Despite this clever replanning of the house, the management of the building contract fell short. The problem was partly Wyatt's fault, for his architectural practice and building business were too big for him to manage properly, and were further undermined by his client. Lord Pembroke, while paying great attention to detail about the work, was absent from Wilton much of the time – in London, and in 1807 travelling as a special envoy to Vienna. During his long absences, Wilton's construction was left under the control of Wyatt's building foremen and clerks of works of variable competence and trustworthiness.

Wyatt had always been disorganised, but, from about 1800, as the correspondence in the Pembroke archive shows, he lost control completely. Part of the problem

The Cloisters inserted into the inner court are Wyatt's major architectural contribution to Wilton, improving the internal communications and adding a distinguished example of late-Georgian, Gothic-revival architecture. The exterior is stuccoed with Parkers Cement, a newly invented product manufactured by James's cousin Charles Wyatt.

Wilton House

James Wyatt's north front, from an old photograph. Wyatt created a new symmetrical north facade at Wilton, which the house had previously lacked. The flanking towers, with pedimented tops added by the 8th Earl, were retained and the walls in between reconstructed with Gothic windows and a central porch. The arms of Henry VIII were reset prominently in the centre over the entrance.

seems to relate to his appointment as Surveyor General of the Office of Works in 1796, in charge of all government and crown buildings, Wyatt used that office's staff in a private capacity and those employees were generally unreliable and occasionally dishonest. There were, however, other problems, not least that Wyatt attempted to act as the building contractor as well as the designer.

Despite the large scale of his practice, Wyatt only earned fees for drawings and attendance and travel expenses. This was not enough to support his lavish way of life: a town house, a country house, six menservants, several carriages and an art collection. So from the late 1790s, he started running the building contracts of the houses he designed, charging an additional 5 percent commission on top of his fees. This extra commitment was eventually to break him, although, at Wilton, everything began well.[2]

In the winter of 1800–1801, Lord Pembroke was enthusiastic about his scheme to convert Wilton into a Gothic abbey with modern conveniences or, as he put it, "Wyatted in good Gothick Taste". Letters from his cousin, the Earl of Caernarvon, trusted that although "a new front will be costly ... Wyatt will imitate the simplicity of old Inigo on the outside and bestow the cash on the Cloysters, Library and Hall". The scheme referred to in this letter had been devised in two sets of sketch plans prepared by Wyatt for Lord Pembroke. The first, made in about 1800, proposed the reconstruction of the north front and a new staircase in the quadrangle, but no cloisters. A more developed sketch on paper watermarked 1801 is essentially the plan executed, with Gothic corridors inserted round the four sides of the old courtyard. These two-storeyed cloisters were built in 1804–05, the lower ones for servants, the upper for sculpture galleries to redisplay the 8th Earl's collection of ancient Roman marbles, and give convenient access to the main rooms. A new central entrance hall at principal floor level and porch were contrived on the north, with various outbuildings on that side demolished and a new forecourt made as the principal approach to

The lower Cloisters are much simpler than the vaulted cloisters on the first floor and were intended as service passages for staff. The brick-built arches along the sides were planned to support the weight of the sculpture displayed upstairs.

the house. The old eastern approach was done away with and the area incorporated into the garden.

In the same design, a dining room was proposed in the former Hunting Room but was not implemented. It was an obvious practical improvement to put the dining room above the servants' hall instead, in the reconstructed north range. The fireplace in this location would heat the dining room above, and also be closer to the new kitchen in part of the riding school building. The Hunting Room was therefore enlarged, repeating Edward Pearce's treatment, to become the billiard room. To create a library, the *sine qua non* of Regency house planning, the whole of the west wing was knocked together and widened to create a single large new room. The first floor of the east wing became the family suite with bed, dressing and sitting rooms for Lord and Lady Pembroke, approached by a new imperial-plan staircase from the Gothic Garden Hall created in the old arched entrance of the Tudor gatehouse, where the outer arch was filled with new glazed doors.

Guest bedrooms were contrived above these family rooms on the east and (for bachelors) on the ground floor under the state rooms on the south. Wyatt's was a brilliant plan, with all the principal rooms on one level approached through the Cloisters. The plan still works today. A new anteroom was created to give access from the Cloisters to the state apartment on the site of the Geometric Stairs which were removed by Wyatt. Like the alterations to the Hunting Room, the Great Anteroom carefully copied "Inigo Jones", and shows how important it was to both Lord Pembroke and Wyatt that the whole sequence of famous seventeenth-century rooms should not be affected by the alterations, and that all the Inigo Jones architecture should be preserved.

James Wyatt was formally appointed architect in 1801, and, in turn, employed Henry Luzmoore (a builder from Carlisle) as clerk of works. Wyatt began in a whirl of enthusiasm, but then paid only one fleeting visit over the next four years. As early as 1802, Lord Pembroke was complaining of delays and threatening to give up the project. A visit from Wyatt in August of that year, along with his charm and the required drawings, calmed things down.

On August 29, 1802, John Seagrim, the agent at Wilton, wrote to Lord Pembroke in London: "Mr. Wyatt left Wilton yesterday evening where he has been stationed for a longer time I understand than he has been at any one time anywhere for some years past, and I have the satisfaction to say to some purpose, for he has determined on every matter contained in the paper of memorandum your Lordship gave me ... It is useless now to say what your Lordship has suffered for want of these instructions before".[3]

The year of 1803 passed without incident or discontent, but there were no visits from Wyatt. Pinnacles and crockets were sent from London. Francis Bernasconi (1762–1841), the stuccoist, started on-site. Bernasconi was the son of a Swiss Italian immigrant, and was the most successful plasterer of the age, used by Wyatt on most of his buildings. But, in 1804, serious complaints again arose, including accusations of dishonesty against Luzmoore, who was then sacked in August that same year. Work ground to a standstill for want of drawings and supervision. The Library was

The Gothic Stairs have a surprisingly simple non-Gothic balustrade. It is possible that the barley-sugar twist wrought-iron banisters were reused from the seventeenth-century Geometric Stairs removed by Wyatt.

The Great Anteroom was created by Wyatt on the site of the Geometric Stairs to give access from the new cloisters to the state rooms. The aim was to match Inigo Jones; the pilasters, cornice, frieze, and doorcase reuse or copy old details.

only half-completed and too narrow, so its outer west wall needed moving outwards several feet, leading to long-term structural defects in the roof, as the supporting beams were extended merely by nailed-on pieces of timber. Lord Pembroke again threatened to give up altogether and dismiss the workforce. A new clerk of works, George Robinson, was appointed, but promptly died.

Then, the year 1805 was punctuated with angry letters from Lord Pembroke to Wyatt accusing the architect of neglect over five years. But, by this time, the east side and the structure of the Cloisters were complete, and Wyatt recommended his cousin, Maria Eginton of Birmingham, to restore and augment Tudor heraldic glass for the traceried windows. Although Wyatt promised to visit Wilton in July, and renewed the promise in August, he didn't turn up until September. This did the trick, and peace was restored for the time being. There were no complaints in 1806. Wyatt came in the autumn and stayed for more than a month, from October 29 until December 8. As a result, work at Wilton proceeded rapidly for a short period. The stained glass in the Cloisters was completed and fixed in patent metal frames in 1807, and the new windows for the Library were sent down from London where they had been made by Wyatt's joiners. The architect himself, no doubt to everybody's gratified amazement, visited four times in 1807, from April 15 to 20, and again in August, October and November. He visited again in May 1808, and a new clerk of works, William Chantry, a mason from the Office of Works, was introduced. Wyatt blamed him for the disasters of the ensuing year, although Lord Pembroke rather took Chantry's side (until he chiselled the surface off an ancient "Greek" altar by mistake).

In 1809, just as the house seemed to be nearing completion, terrible defects emerged in all the new work. The Library's flue set fire to the Cloisters the first time it was used, the new floors were found to be infected with dry rot, and the stucco in the Cloisters, cracked and fell off. Lord Pembroke complained of "extreme and I should suppose unexampled negligence which has caused me injury by unnecessarily long progress of works, most of which have proved so defective as to need entire rebuilding."

Part of the problem at Wilton was caused by the unreliability of the men Wyatt appointed to run the contract on-site. The architect's absenteeism and intermittent enthusiasm would not have been so deleterious if there had been the continuous management of a good clerk of works who knew what to do and could interpret Wyatt's architectural intentions. At Wilton both William Chantry, the clerk of works, and Edward Crocker, Wyatt's peripatetic surveyor for measuring and costing building work, had both previously worked together on the new Speaker's House at the Palace of Westminster, one of Wyatt's official jobs as Surveyor of the Office of Works. Chantry and Crocker hated each other, and their mutual distrust was at the root of the problems that developed at Wilton in 1809–10. William Chantry accused Crocker of dishonesty to Lord Pembroke, and claimed he was taking backhanders from the workmen. So there may have been financial irregularity as well as practical incompetence during the last two years of Wyatt's building contract. Wyatt blamed Chantry for the mistakes and delays and thought Chantry was blackguarding him behind his back. He told Lord Pembroke that "your Lordship's mind has been

opposite The ceiling of the Great Anteroom was painted in 1816 in the spirit of the French artist Andien de Clermont, with a sky and balustrade by Thomas Ward, the Regency decorator.

following pages The west side of the Cloisters seen through Wyatt's stone traceried perpendicular windows. The east bay window in the Cloisters and sixteenth-century heraldic glass cartouches are displayed as part of Wyatt's design by his cousin Maria Eginton of Birmingham, who restored and augmented them.

left The south side of the Cloisters showing Wyatt's arrangement of the 8th Earl's antique busts on the mid-seventeenth-century marble pedestals made in Rome for Cardinal Mazarin.

below left The west side of the Cloisters. The chimneypiece is a recent copy of the unusual arrangement contrived by Wyatt to display sculpture. The Cloisters were intended as dedicated galleries for the 8th Earl's classical sculpture collection, previously disposed throughout the state rooms.

opposite The north side of the Cloisters. The arrangement survives largely as devised by the sculptor Sir Richard Westmacott, a family friend of Wyatt's whom the architect introduced to restore and display the busts and statues, mainly from the Mazarin Collection. The stone plinths with inset marble reliefs were designed by Wyatt and made by William Chantry, the clerk of works, who caused a great upset by acting on his own to clean off with a claw hammer the background surface of the first-century Greco-Roman Bacchic altar.

The north Cloisters with the Wyatt-Westmacott arrangement of sculptures. The altar "tidied" by poor William Chantry is on the left. Wyatt's projecting corbels were too small to hold most of the busts in the collection, one of the reasons why the 11th Earl of Pembroke retained Westmacott to reorganise the sculpture display after Wyatt's dismissal and death.

poisoned against me (foolishly and impertinently so). I am convinced from some circumstances which had occurred before I was last at Wilton and during my stay there".[4] With all these personal rows erupting, after nine years of a rackety building contract, it is hardly surprising that Lord Pembroke had had enough, and terminated the whole project. After considerable expenditure, and despite the beauty of some of the new work, he was left with a house that lacked a kitchen, and had an incomplete main entrance and forecourt, defective chimneys, defective drains, dry rot, cracking plaster and a collapsing ceiling in the library. Meanwhile the valuable collection of ancient sculpture, one of the special treasures of Wilton, which had been removed from the old great hall and the west wing when they were demolished, was lying haphazardly outside, barely protected from the weather and the careless workmen, whose tools damaged the sculpture. John Seagrim, Lord Pembroke's agent at Wilton, had summed up correctly as early as 1805: "I give Mr. Wyatt full credit for his [artistic] abilities" but it was a mistake to have employed him "for planning and supervising"[5] the work rather than using a local building contractor.

Meanwhile, James Wyatt fell seriously ill, not leaving his bedroom for two months during the summer of 1809. In addition, his finances collapsed, and he appointed a lawyer friend, Mr. James of New Inn, and his eldest son, Benjamin Dean Wyatt (1775–1852), to sort things out. Benjamin, who acted as his father's architectural assistant, lacked James's charm and tactlessly aggravated the situation by choosing to send Lord Pembroke a large bill on April 13, 1809, for back payment of his father's fees and commission: "Unless my Father should be enabled to collect a very large sum of money on or before the 25th of this month, he must incur a very serious and painful degree of embarrassment".[6]

With grim satisfaction, Lord Pembroke sent back a stinging rejoinder, refusing to pay until various defects had been put right, and until essential working drawings were dispatched to Wilton. This caused Wyatt himself to write a long letter of explanation and excuse. The architect, despite the chaos of the long-drawn-out works, the incomplete and uncomfortable state of the house, the uncontrolled expense and the gathering fury on all sides, seems to have been genuinely surprised by Lord Pembroke's final ultimatum, and reacted with astonishment and hurt feelings: "The letter which I had the honour to receive from your Lordship ... has equally hurt and surprised me – I could not have conceived it possible that you should have entertained the sentiments and opinions in that letter relative to the works at Wilton House, because I flattered myself (and I am sure not without reason) that your Lordship as well as many of your friends were not only highly pleased with all that has been done there, but have frequently join'd your Lordship in expressing to a degree of astonishment their surprise at the improvements which have been made at Wilton under my direction".[7] Lord Pembroke was not to be appeased. He again refused payment, citing "the fault and dangerous execution" of the work. This correspondence continued all through August and September, when Lord Pembroke agreed to pay Wyatt a reduced sum on condition that he send all the drawings required for completing the house. By December, a terrible stench from the new drains signalled yet another defect in the new building.

Lord Pembroke finally sent Wyatt a payment of £1,500 on account of fees in January 1810, but was still complaining about the state of the house and requiring Wyatt's immediate attendance at Wilton. Then, in February, he decided to dispense with Wyatt's supervisory services, but demanded that Wyatt provide all the working drawings still due (for the chapel, forecourt and kitchen offices) as soon as possible, and with no further charge. Wyatt obliged and, in 1810, amazingly visited Wilton on

no fewer than five occasions. By April 1810, costs had reached £50,000, not including Wyatt's fees, so Lord Pembroke finally lost patience and sacked the whole work-force. The house was completed, and redecorated, by Lord Pembroke's dynamic young second wife, Catherine Woronzow (1784–1856), daughter of the Russian ambassador. They had married in 1808. She turned out to be an excellent manager, and the perfect châtelaine for Wilton. She worked effectively, with the help of Sir Richard Westmacott as sculptor, architect and decorator, and Money Fisher the latest clerk of works, as the builder, to complete the kitchen offices, stables and entrance court. Fisher was a local man from Salisbury, unlike his predecessors from Carlisle and London, and proved able and efficient. He later became clerk of works to Salisbury Cathedral.

left Sir Thomas Lawrence, *Catherine Woronzow, Countess of Pembroke*. Woronzow was the daughter of Count Simon Woronzow, Russian ambassador in London.

right William Owen, *George Augustus, 11th Earl of Pembroke*. He employed James Wyatt from 1800 to 1810 to replan Wilton and to rebuild the north and west sides of the house.

The aesthetic quality of Wyatt's work at Wilton is difficult to judge now, as most of it was removed in the twentieth century for reasons of taste as well as structural inadequacy. Old photographs, however, hardly make the pulse race, with their sepia views of large rooms replete with mechanical Gothic detail. However, the Cloisters are splendid both inside and out. Their plaster vaults (by Bernasconi) and traceried and oriel windows make them a landmark in the Gothic Revival. As an architect, Wyatt's great achievement at Wilton remains the plan, which resolved the different floor levels of the old building in a masterly way and contrived a convenient and commodious modern house. The convincing-looking ribs of the lierne vaults, the corbel, and the bosses in the new Cloisters and Gothic Hall were moulded from plaster casts of sections of genuine medieval vaults that Wyatt had commissioned Bernasconi to make for him during the restoration of Lichfield and Hereford Cathedrals. Wyatt also used them in his Gothic work at Oxford, including New College, Balliol and Magdalen, where he restored the college halls and chapel.

James Wyatt's dismissal in 1810, as has been described, followed angry correspondence from Lord Pembroke,[8] and the contract ended with the client and architect

opposite The north-west corner of the Cloisters. Wyatt's plan was to place the Roman sarcophagi on axis at the ends of the Cloister vistas, and to place busts on Gothic corbels. This sarcophagus from the Via Appia is supported, as intended by Wyatt, on two sections cut from an antique Roman column of granite.

above The north-east corner of the Cloisters as intended by Wyatt, with another of the Via Appia sarcophagi flanked by restored second-century statues of a fawn with panther and Cupid stringing his bow, from the Mazarin Collection.

opposite above The Images Bridge, designed by Sir Richard Westmacott to display the statues by Nicholas Stone of Flora and Bacchus from the 4th Earl of Pembroke's garden. The statues were deemed too large for the Cloisters.

opposite below The Echo Seat, designed by Sir Richard Westmacott. All the area to the east of the house was added to the garden after the creation of Wyatt's north forecourt and the eradication of the 8th Earl's former entrance arrangement. The seat terminates a long gravel walk on the axis of the Tudor gate tower.

above The "Orchid House", designed by Sir Richard Westmacott as an open loggia overlooking the new Italian garden, incorporates the marble reliefs by Nicholas Stone from the 4th Earl's grotto.

The Italian Garden laid out in the 1820s to the west of the house by Catherine Woronzow and centred on the 2nd Earl's Elizabethan fountain, originally in the inner court.

barely on speaking terms. For the next year, however, Wyatt continued to provide drawings for completing the house, including plans for the north forecourt and the kitchen offices fitted into one end of the 10th Earl's mid-eighteenth-century riding school, the best practical solution but aesthetically regrettable. When Catherine Woronzow took over the direction of Wilton's works for her husband, she coordinated all of Wyatt's designs, chose the sculpture to be displayed in the Cloisters, and decorated and furnished the rooms including rehanging the pictures.[9] Richard Westmacott, who had been introduced by Wyatt to arrange the sculpture in the Cloisters, stayed on for another fifteen years, assisting Lady Pembroke. He also acted as a de facto interior decorator, designing furniture, down to the curtains, as well as the garden buildings that included stone seats, bridges, loggias and an orangery. He contributed other architectural features, such as reconstructing the Holbein Porch in the West Garden in 1826, and placing Peter Scheemakers' Shakespeare statue there. It had been displaced by the demolition of the Geometric Stairs. The interior of the house was transformed into a cross between a comfortable English country house and a Continental palace, the "Inigo Jones" state rooms, a blaze of crimson and gold, furnished with Chippendale pieces and gilded William Kent furniture, introduced in the 1820s by Catherine, and a degree of formality in the enlarged gardens to the east and west, all with Richard Westmacott's help.

In the eighteenth century, under the 8th, 9th and 10th Earls, the state rooms at Wilton contained very little furniture, as opposed to works of art. The Cube and Double Cube Rooms were furnished only with pier tables, introduced by Henry, the 9th Earl, stools and ancient classical busts on Cardinal Mazarin's marble, polychrome pedestals. There was not even a bed in the King's Bedroom. When George III visited in 1778 a bed was borrowed from William Beckford's nearby Wiltshire seat, Fonthill Splendens, although in the event, as has been seen, this proved unnecessary as the King brought a travelling bed with him. The rooms were now richly arranged by Catherine and Westmacott, with gilt and crimson furniture attributed to Chippendale and William Kent, and other new pieces made to match. Although highly appropriate and until recently assumed to have been made for the house in the eighteenth century, none of these pieces are indigenous to Wilton; rather, they represent a grand historicist Regency scheme carried out between 1811 and the 1820s.

The Chippendale furniture, commissioned by Henry, the 10th Earl, was made for Pembroke House, Whitehall; it was brought to Wilton when that house was let in the early nineteenth century and finally given up on the death of George, the 11th Earl of Pembroke, in 1827. The gilded Kent and Kent-style pieces came to Wilton only in the 1820s. This furniture had been made for the Earl of Tilney's family seat at Wanstead House in Essex and was dispersed in a much publicised sale of 1822 which preceded the sad 1824 demolition of that Palladian palace, designed by Colin Campbell. Peter Brown (director of Fairfax House, York) was the first to identify the famous set of six William Kent settees and a set of gilt chairs at Wilton as coming from Wanstead, as they are depicted *in situ* in eighteenth-century portraits of the Tilney family sitting in the saloon and drawing room at Wanstead. The catalogue of the Wanstead sale showed that not just those pieces but also most of the gilt Kentian

The Sphynx and Diana settees in the state rooms were designed by William Kent for Wansted House in Essex, the seat of the Earl of Tilney; six of the settees, along with other carved and gilt furniture, were acquired for Wilton at the Wansted sale in 1822, prior to the demolition of that Palladian palace.

furniture at Wilton came from Wanstead. Catherine also collected some glamorous Continental furniture to enhance the state rooms, including Boulle writing tables and clocks, French commodes, and a gilt fire screen, said to be of French royal provenance. These French acquisitions are representative of English nineteenth-century taste, when such items were copiously available following the upheavals of the French Revolution.

below left Detail of the velvet curtains in the Single Cube Room, showing tassels and passementerie, part of Catherine Woronzow's redecoration and furnishing of the state rooms in the 1820s.

above right Design for the curtains in the Double Cube Room by Sir Richard Westmacott. The 11th Earl and his wife, Catherine, were so pleased with Westmacott's arrangement of the sculpture in the Cloisters that they employed him for a further ten years as architect, decorator and garden designer.

After Wyatt left, the work on Wilton entered a new, more dynamic phase with the completion, decoration and furnishing of the interiors. The house was largely completed by Catherine, Lady Pembroke herself, working into the 1820s. She had strong aesthetic tastes and was to remain in charge at Wilton for the next forty years, even after her husband's death in 1827. Not all the accounts survive, and there are, for example, no records of payments for the Wanstead furniture, but Catherine's notebooks, many sketch ideas, picture-hanging plans and some bills survive in the family archives, together with designs by Sir Richard Westmacott and James Wyatt's nephew Jeffry Wyatt (subsequently Wyatville), more famous as George IV's architect at Windsor Castle, and later, Thomas Henry Wyatt, the grandson of James's eldest

brother William Wyatt. So James's disappearance from the scene was by no means the end of the Wyatts at Wilton. Sir Jeffry Wyatville designed the Chinese Breakfast Room, on the ground floor of the south-west tower, replacing the 9th Earl's bath. Later, Thomas Henry Wyatt designed the dairy, fitted up the interior of the chapel and created the basilican parish church of St. Mary in the town in the 1840s for Catherine and her son Sidney Herbert, later Lord Herbert of Lea (1810–1861).

Catherine got to work the moment Wyatt left the scene. A notebook annotated "CW 1810" contains "the dimensions at Wilton for furnishing" and another folder contains partial accounts for the work up to 1828. In 1811 Robertson & Burton of Oxford Street supplied brass inlaid mahogany library chairs. These are the set now in the Large Smoking Room (one of which is inscribed "Burton" in pencil underneath). Two Gothic mahogany desks were also provided for the Library; designed by James Wyatt, they matched the original architecture of the room, which had four-centred Perpendicular arches and a coffered and oak-grained plaster ceiling (all remodelled around 1930 in classical taste). The new bedrooms seem to have been decorated by London firms, such as Bloomsbury Upholsterers, which provided beds, and Edward Reeder, which supplied textiles for curtains in the early nineteenth century.

In 1811, Thomas Ward, the well-known Regency painter-decorator (responsible for graining the library at Nostell Priory, Yorkshire), was paid for gilding in the Colonnade Room and painting the ceiling of Wyatt's Great Anteroom with sky trellis and roses. Westmacott made a small gilt plaster copy of Rysbrack's statue of Inigo Jones (at Chiswick House) to stand on the chimneypiece of the Great Anteroom, which is, also in its classical architecture, a tribute to Jones, having been designed by James Wyatt as the new access to the state rooms from the Cloisters. The Hunting Room in the south-west tower, which had been enlarged by Wyatt, was also decorated by Ward with a similar painted sky ceiling to that in the Great Anteroom, and furnished as the billiard room. A bedroom above was hung with "Blue Star Paper". The breakfast room below was created around 1814 to Wyatville's design on the site of the 9th Earl's bath, and has been remarked on. The room was hung with blue-ground Chinese paper and furnished with inbuilt glazed cases with faux bamboo frames to display Chinese porcelain, in a set piece of Regency Brighton Pavilion taste, popularised by King George IV.

In 1816, Catherine Woronzow set to work with Sir Richard Westmacott on the redisplay of the 8th Earl's collection of classical sculpture in the new entrance hall, and the Cloisters, where Wyatt's scheme was incomplete and in any case was not acceptable to the Pembrokes as it omitted most of the statues. Wyatt had proposed installing the six largest statues in the entrance hall with four busts of philosophers in between, all on square stone plinths made by the clerk of works, William Chantry, in 1809. In the Cloisters, Wyatt proposed placing the sarcophagi over the east and west chimneypieces and at the ends of the vistas, flanked on each side by statues. He also designed pretty Gothic corbels high up along the walls for busts and inserted the marble reliefs between them at the same height. Along the sides, he intended to rearrange the classical busts to sit on the marble pedestals on which they had been displayed in Cardinal Mazarin's collection in Paris, and in the state rooms at Wilton

opposite and previous page
The North Hall, designed by James Wyatt in 1809, and intended as the new main entrance at principal floor level, from the new north forecourt. Wyatt and Lord Pembroke intended the hall to display the historic armour and the largest Roman statues in the collection. The statue of Apollo is one of the most important at Wilton. It was excavated in Rome and given by Cardinal Ottoboni to King Louis XIV of France, intended for the Château de Marly. After the king's death in 1714, it was acquired by the 8th Earl. The 9th Earl's statue of Shakespeare carved by Peter Scheemakers to the design of William Kent, moved from the Geometric Stairs, has found an appropriate resting place as the central focus of the hall.

in the eighteenth-century, following their acquisition by the 8th Earl of Pembroke.

George, the 11th Earl of Pembroke, explained in an interesting letter to Richard Westmacott in July 1812 why he and his wife, Catherine, wanted the arrangement changing, where practicable. The corbels were too high for any busts placed on them to be seen properly and were too small to hold most of the busts in the collection. The reliefs were also too high to be seen, but impossible to move "without taking the place to pieces", so they would have to stay. The Roman sarcophagi had

right The French boulle clock in the Single Cube Room is one of Catherine Woronzow's furnishings and typical of early nineteenth-century English taste led by George IV, when such objects were available in the aftermath of the French Revolution. The bronze figures are the seventeenth-century firedogs from the Double Cube Room.

opposite The great doorcase in the Double Cube Room. The double doors with circular central panels replace the seventeenth-century originals with rectangular panels. They were designed by Westmacott for Catherine Woronzow in the 1820s.

also been placed and were too heavy to move again. The entrance hall, the north-east, south-east and south-west angles and the fireplaces were to "remain as intended by Mr. Wyatt". But Lord Pembroke wanted centrepiece statues flanked by busts in each bay along the sides of the Cloisters. As a result, most of the corbels designed by Wyatt were never used for their original purpose.[10]

Westmacott – under Catherine Woronzow's supervision – rearranged all the sculpture accordingly, on the basis of sketches that she had approved. One is anno-tated in her forceful script "too crowded", while another subject was considered "not proper" to place in a prominent position. She was concerned not just to achieve a picturesque arrangement of the statuary, but also to improve the quality of the collection on display, wanting to show the best antique pieces to advantage. Her notebooks, for instance, included a list of sculpture that had been "condemned on the authority of Jenkins" – a reference to Thomas Jenkins (1722–1798), the celebrated British dealer in classical sculpture in late eighteenth-century Rome, who had been one of the first "experts" to call some of the Wilton antique statuary "fake".

The collaboration with Westmacott of the Cloisters was such a success that Catherine then used him to help with furnishing the Single Cube and Double Cube Rooms. Work there got underway in the 1820s. A London firm of upholsterers, Duke & Son, supplied red velvet curtains with white satin linings and gold gimp and trim in 1823. Westmacott provided new doors with circular central panels on the French model to replace the seventeenth-century rectangular panelled origi-nals. These new doors, now painted white and gold, were intended to be grained to represent rosewood. Another painter, George Whitmarsh, was paid for regilding the room in 1824–26. This had only just been completed when Lord Pembroke died in 1827, and the fully furnished rooms are recorded in the inventory made at the time of his death. The impetus for this splendid refurbishment was obviously the arrival of the Wanstead furniture following its sale in 1822. How this was acquired is not recorded, but there can be no doubt of its provenance, as it closely matches the descriptions in the sale catalogue.

The furniture introduced into the Double Cube Room at Wilton included not just six of the Kent settees from the saloon at Wanstead, but also a set of eight large easy chairs, or "state fauteuils" from the Great Drawing Room, and a pair of large sofas with earls' coronets on their backs from the Grand Hall at Wanstead. The set of "back stools" from the Wanstead drawing room, are now in the Single Cube Room at Wilton. Other Wanstead pieces include the daybed and possibly the boulle desks in the Colonnade Room.[11]

Additional matching pieces for Wilton were designed by Westmacott, with some of his sketches surviving. The white and gold "dolphin consoles" with marble tops and octagonal central table *en suite* were designed by him, as were two large gilt torchère stands with kneeling Hercules figures, now in the library, but intended for the Double Cube Room. The huge gilt sofa under the great Van Dyck family piece in the Double Cube Room was probably also designed by Westmacott but no sketches by him survive for that. He also designed the pier glass in the Single Cube Room and the pelmets incorporating Chippendale carvings from Pembroke House, as well as

One of a pair of pedestals with kneeling Atlas figures. They were designed by Westmacott for the Double Cube Room, and are now in the Library.

curtains of crimson Genoa velvet in both the Single and Double Cube Rooms. All this was done in close cooperation with Catherine and some of the drawings are inscribed in her hand. "Mr. Westmacott's design". Existing records give the impression of a strong client and an amenable sculptor-artist working together to create a theatrical-historical, palatial ensemble of crimson, white and gold around the furniture acquired from Wanstead, with other pieces of suitable scale and richness added to match. The Pembrokes and Westmacott obviously got on well and were of like minds; otherwise it is difficult to imagine a sculptor of Westmacott's distinction spending time on the design of curtains and the like.

The smaller state rooms, originally the king's apartment, Colonnade Room (King's Bed Chamber), Corner Room (King's Dressing Room) and Little Anteroom (King's Closet), had been decorated around 1811, immediately after James Wyatt was dismissed, when Thomas Ward, the decorator, was paid for painting and gilding. The original crimson flock paper in the dressing room and closet (now replaced with a copy of the faded and damaged original) was stamped H and watermarked 1811. When Pembroke House was given up in 1827, the carved Chippendale pelmets from there were placed in these rooms, and further paintings integrated into revised tiered picture hangs. Sketch elevations survive of the walls with moveable pieces of paper to scale, to assist in planning the position of the paintings, especially in the closet and dressing room, which had always been small picture galleries. The dressing room had been called "the Cabinet" by Inigo Jones on his ceiling design for the rooms, showing that it was intended to be hung with small paintings from the beginning. Today those two rooms contain some of the paintings given to the 5th Earl in 1669 by Cosimo III, Grand Duke of Tuscany, including a version of Titian's *Magdalen*, an Andrea del Sarto *Virgin and Child* and a poetic portrait of a *Shepherd* once attributed to Giorgione, as well as choice Flemish and Italian works from the 8th Earl's collection, of which *Leda and the Swan* by a pupil of Leonardo da Vinci is the most striking.

After her husband, George Pembroke, died in 1827, Catherine Woronzow, Lady Pembroke, continued to live at Wilton. The couple's son, Sidney, later Lord Herbert of Lea, was famous as a supporter of Florence Nightingale and Secretary for War during the Crimea in 1856 (ironic, as he was half Russian), rented Wilton from his elder half-brother Robert, the 12th Earl, who lived his life in Paris, having been disinherited for marrying a Sicilian adventuress during his Grand Tour, without his father's permission. Catherine then used the corner rooms as her own comfortable sitting rooms. The Double and Single Cubes were used as drawing rooms and silted up with extra furniture and bric-a-brac, as recorded in Victorian photographs. In the twentieth century, the state rooms were thinned out, and the picture hangs revised, but all of the Wanstead and Westmacott furniture and decoration has survived. This essentially Regency scheme adds a special dimension to the seventeenth-century architecture and is so convincing that most twentieth-century scholars assumed that the rooms had been refurnished by William Kent in the 1730s for his friend Henry, the 9th Earl (the two had met on the Grand Tour in Rome), thus contributing a further layer to the Wilton Myth.

The chimneypiece in the King's Closet (Little Anteroom) was supplied by Westmacott, and his design for it survives in the archives.

Catherine Woronzow and Sidney Herbert, the Tory statesman, continued to run Wilton as it had been in the 11th Earl of Pembroke's time. Sidney was created a peer in his own right as Lord Herbert of Lea. On the death of his elder half-brother Robert, the 12th Earl, without legitimate children, in 1862, Wilton was inherited by Sidney's eldest son George as the 13th Earl of Pembroke. George and his younger brother, the 14th Earl, made few architectural changes to the house in the second half of the nineteenth century, admiring their grandmother's work, and concentrating their energies on building model farms and cottages on the wider estate. George, the 13th Earl, followed his father, Lord Herbert of Lea, into Parliament, and was undersecretary for war in Disraeli's government in 1874. He was

opposite The King's Dressing Room (Corner Room) was decorated by Catherine Woronzow with a Pavia-pattern, crimson flock wallpaper in a seventeenth-century-style and watermarked 1811 (replaced in replica 2017). Catherine placed here carved and gilt rococo window cornices for the curtains that had been made for the 10th Earl by Chippendale for Pembroke House, Whitehall, which was given up as the family's London house by the 11th Earl.

left Sir Francis Grant, Sidney, Lord Herbert of Lea, with his red box as Secretary of State for War, son of the 11th Earl and Catherine Woronzow. After his father's death, Sidney rented Wilton from his half-brother, Robert, the 12th Earl, who had quarrelled with his father and spent his life in Paris. Sidney's two sons, Robert and Sidney, inherited the earldom in turn and lived at Wilton into the twentieth century, keeping it much as it had been completed and furnished by their grandmother, Catherine.

a trustee of the National Portrait Gallery and a member of the Roxburghe Club, the preeminent English society of bibliophiles. Like his father, Lord Herbert of Lea, George also took a special interest in the Fitzwilliam estate in Dublin which the 11th Earl had inherited in 1811 from a distant cousin. The Irish estate came to the Pembroke family from the last Viscount Fitzwilliam (in the Irish peerage) who founded the Fitzwilliam Museum in Cambridge to house his art collection. He also bequeathed funds to help build the gallery, and to support his old university, but he left his other property to his Herbert relations. This Irish property, which included extensive ground rents in Dublin, helped underpin Victorian Wilton and augmented the agricultural income from the Wiltshire estate, especially in the late nineteenth century when English farm rents declined. Lord Herbert and his sons took an interest in the Dublin estate and invested in it. In Booterstown Dublin in 1850, Lord Herbert of Lea built the Romanesque Revival Church of Ireland St. John's, designed by the architect Benjamin Ferrey (1810–1880), a pupil of A. W. N. Pugin. He also built St. Bartholomew's Church in Ballsbridge, just as he and his mother Catherine Woronzow had built St. Mary's Church at Wilton. The latter church was an imposing neo-Italianate basilica designed by Thomas Henry Wyatt in the 1840s. Catherine and Sidney filled it with Continental works of art – French medieval glass, rare marbles and Italian Cosmati work. Catherine and Sidney Herbert were both High Church Anglicans and strongly religious. Sidney's wife, Elizabeth à Court (1822–1911), became a famous Victorian convert to Catholicism and a friend of Cardinal Manning, the Oxford Movement prelate who was Catholic Archbishop of Westminster. Elizabeth Herbert was also a prolific author whose books reflect her strong religious faith. Sidney Herbert built churches and supported religious charities, while his son, George, the 13th Earl, built and endowed the Pembroke Technical College in Ringsend, Dublin, in 1892. The design competition was won by William Kaye-Parry (1853–1932), the Dublin architect. Lord Pembroke himself laid the foundation stone. This patronage of religious and educational buildings was typical of the social improvement policies of conscientious, public-spirited Victorian landowners, of which the Herberts were prominent examples.

After George Pembroke died of tuberculosis in 1895, he was succeeded by his younger brother, another Sidney, as 14th Earl. Sidney had also served as a Conservative MP and was an active courtier at the turn of the twentieth century, serving as Lord Steward of the Royal Household in the last years of Queen Victoria's reign, and under King Edward VII. Although neither the 13th nor the 14th Earls made architectural alterations at Wilton, their occupation of the house in the late-Victorian and Edwardian years was a golden age, with the place once more a focus of contemporary social and cultural life. The earl's sister Constance (1859–1917) married Earl de Grey, later the 2nd Marquess of Ripon (1852–1923), the famous Edwardian shot and friend of the Prince of Wales, later Edward VII. Constance Ripon was a patron of the arts, friend of Oscar Wilde and Dame Nellie Melba, and one of the great society hostesses of the period. Wilton was also renowned at that time for its large house parties, with King Edward VII and Queen Alexandra coming to stay in 1908. Modern bathroom plumbing was installed for the king and queen's visit, as was also the case at Chatsworth. Queen Alexandra took a photograph of the east front of Wilton with the Tudor gatehouse, which still survives in the family albums.[12]

The family circle of the 13th and 14th Earls also contained many interesting and talented people. The earl's younger brother, Sir Michael Herbert (1857–1903), was the British ambassador in Washington, DC. Their eldest sister Mary (1849–1935) married the Anglo-Viennese Catholic theologian and biblical commentator Baron Friedrich von Hügel (1852–1925), while their middle sister Elizabeth married the leading composer Sir Hubert Parry (1848–1918), who wrote the anthem "For I Was Glad" for the coronation of Edward VII. The death of Sidney, the 14th Earl of Pembroke, in Rome in 1913 marked the end of a social, political and cultural "Indian summer" at Wilton, and also ended a century of architectural stability in the history of the house. Reginald, Sidney's eldest son, who inherited as the 15th Earl of Pembroke in 1913, immediately embarked on a new campaign of alteration and remodelling, partly aimed at removing what had come to be seen by that date to be the worst blemishes of Wyatt's work. It was a campaign which was to continue until the end of the twentieth century, despite two World Wars and the economic disruptions caused by Civil War in Ireland, the General Strike in 1926, the great economic crash in 1929 and decades of socialist high taxation in Britain.

The story of Wilton in the twentieth century is not the least interesting part of its history, and demonstrates the remarkable resilience of the English aristocracy and the country house despite the emergence of political and economic forces that might have been expected to overwhelm and obliterate both. At Wilton, the story of the survival, restoration and embellishment of the house is one of remarkable devotion, and a tribute to the strength of the unique Wilton "Myth" and its ability to inspire and sustain successive generations of owners to live in and care for the house as their ancestors had done.

Chapter Five
Restoration and Revival

THE NORTH FORECOURT AT WILTON HOUSE WAS REMODELLED IN 1971 BY THE
decorator-gardener David Vicary as a memorial to Sidney, 16th Earl of Pembroke
(1906–1969). The design with pleached limes, box-edged beds of tulips, lavender,
standard honeysuckle and roses is arranged around a central fountain pool. The
encircling plinth of Portland Stone has a carved inscription that reads: "This forecourt was laid out by his son Henry, to remember the life of Sidney, sixteenth Earl of
Pembroke, connoisseur, historian and countryman, who lived from 9 January 1906
to 16 March 1969 – a lifetime given in devotion to Wilton House". This encapsulates
the spirit in which four successive generations of the Pembroke family have restored
and further embellished the house over the last hundred years. Much of this work is
recorded in notes kept by the 16th Earl explaining his and his father's alterations to
the house between 1913, when his grandfather died, and the 1960s, when he carried
out his own programme. A quotation will give a flavour of the notes. It is interesting
and unusual to have such a contemporary description of alterations to a historic
house compiled by the owner.

*After my Grandfather died in 1913, my Father decided to alter the north front at Wilton,
built in the "Sham" gothic style by James Wyatt between 1801 and 1814, the ivy covered
porch to the front door was removed; the tall pointed windows, with stained glass at
the top which existed between the towers of the north front, and which were the Wyatt
dining room windows on the right and bedrooms on the left were taken out when
the main walls between the towers were reconstructed. Edmund [sic] Warre was the
architect chosen for all this; the idea was to make the north front between the towers look
more like it was thought to have been before the Wyatt alterations. But Warre did not do
this, and put in windows of different height and levels, with small glass panes in Tudor
style, which look very silly. The central front door tower was rebuilt, and the carved*

stone balcony over the front door, which is quite effective, was made. Stone balustrades were made along the edge of the roof and on the ground level.

The Wyatt dining room to the right or west of the front door, was decorated in shoulder high brown plaster made to look like panelling and was hideous and dark; it occupied, together with the Wyatt front hall, the site of the sixteenth-century Great Hall .... The inside of the dining room was completely altered; the ceiling was lowered some twelve feet, and a passage and two bedrooms were built over it. The door from the cloisters into it ... was blocked out, and a new one with double doors made in the centre of the room. The caryatids and over-door which are of the Inigo Jones-Webb period had been found in the sawmills, and were put in, and the tapestries which had been found rolled up under the sun blinds in the Library, were placed on the west and east wall in the specially constructed new decoration scheme, and the two very large paintings by Reynolds, ... were placed on either side of the double doors. The entire decoration of the room was carried out in a blue-green and white colour. This was done in 1919 after all the structural work had been completed, which had begun in 1914, and went on all through the war, although the house was in use as a hospital, because the stonemasons and bricklayers were all too old to fight, and no ban on buildings operations such as this appears to have been enforced at that time ...

At the same time as the re-building, the drains which were in a very bad condition, were entirely replaced and extended. The house was also wired for electric light, but the War broke out while this was being done, and it was not finished, nor did the engine which was to make it (in the sawmills) arrive, so that the hospital for Officers which my mother organised and ran as Commandant till 1918, had to manage with gas, and oil lamps. Electricity was finally working in 1919. Central heating was also installed on a moderate scale at this time and has been increased since, and overhauled several times, and oil fired boilers put in.

Up to 1913, there were very few bathrooms ... For King Edward VII's visit with Queen Alexandra in 1908, the bathroom to the north of my grandfather's bedroom was specially made. After 1913, bathrooms were put in, but not all at once, South West tower (three), Maiden Lane (three), the north passage for maids (one), the north bedrooms, then called the Bugle rooms (one), the menservants rooms below (one), Bachelor's Row (three), South West tower (three), Nursery tower (two), Flagstaff tower (one), Clock tower (one), back passage and men's rooms (two)....[1]

Reginald, the 15th Earl of Pembroke (1880–1960), who succeeded his father in 1913, married Lady Beatrice Paget, the sister of the 6th Marquess of Anglesey (1885–1947). Her family was keenly interested in beautiful old houses, and remodelled their principal Tudor seat at Beaudesert in Staffordshire in the Edwardian period, and then Plas Newydd, their Welsh seat on the Isle of Anglesey in the 1920s and 1930s, and these campaigns helped stimulate the remodelling of Wilton in which Beatrice Pembroke took a strong interest, later aided and abetted by her sons Sidney and David Herbert. The Pembrokes and the Angleseys were part of the family circles of cultivated Edwardians known as the "Souls" who shared literary and aesthetic interests. The circles also included the Manners family (Dukes of Rutland) at Haddon,

Derbyshire, the Charteris family (Earls of Wemyss) at Stanway, Gloucestershire, and the Lindsays, Earls of Crawford, and their many artistic cousins. The Pembrokes' aim was to remodel Wyatt's north and west sides of the house containing the Library and Dining Room and to bring these more closely into harmony with the beautiful seventeenth-century Jonesian parts of the house. These works at Wilton add a significant twentieth-century architectural element to the art history of the house. In addition to the remodelled north entrance front, the twentieth-century phase created two especially impressive interiors that complement the Inigo Jones/John Webb state rooms in the south range.

The remodelling begun in 1913 is the work and major achievement of a young Edwardian architect, Edmond Lancelot "Bear" Warre (1877–1961), whose early promise was blighted by the First World War, as few of his circle of clients were inclined to undertake new architectural projects of the same scale after the war. However, he did go on to design Glyndebourne Opera House in Sussex for the Christies in the 1930s.

Embarking on the major reconstruction of a historic house such as Wilton in 1913 – on the eve of the First World War – seems rather odd in retrospect, but to those living at the time, the future looked rosy: the Lloyd George threat (of land taxes)

An aerial photograph shows Wilton's north forecourt with David Vicary's memorial garden to Sidney, 16th Earl of Pembroke, who died in 1969. The design celebrates his "lifetime given in devotion to Wilton House", with its pleached limes, box-edged garden beds and circular pool. The 10th Earl's Riding School is on the right.

had been averted; the economy was booming; the stock market had reached record heights. Many other great houses saw similar ambitious architectural schemes initiated in the same years, notably Chatsworth for the Duke of Devonshire, and Knowsley for the Earl of Derby – where the architect, W. H. Romaine Walker (1854–1940) was responsible for pre–First World War campaigns of "restoration to what never existed", to quote Lord Derby. James Wyatt's two Gothic wings of 1800–1810, carried out for George, the 11th Earl of Pembroke, were almost universally despised at the beginning of the twentieth century. "Dull", "unimpressive", "bathos" were terms applied. Critics thought that "Wyatt the Destroyer" had demolished Tudor-Renaissance and Inigo Jones elevations and interiors to make way for "hideous sham Gothic" unworthy of the seventeenth-century south front and state rooms, and the mid-sixteenth-century gatehouse on the east side.[2]

It was determined, therefore, to return Wyatt's north front and interiors to the condition in which they might have been before they succumbed to "misguided" Regency meddling. The Edwardian remodelling was in fact based on a mistaken premise. The quadrangular house at Wilton had never had north and west façades prior to Wyatt. The former rooms in those wings were piecemeal Georgian remodellings of Tudor spaces and were lit mainly by windows facing into the inner courtyard. The old north and west exteriors were largely unfenestrated and irregular as has been seen, with the projecting chapel on the west side and a plethora of "out-offices", backyards and the semidetached kitchen impinging directly on to the town to the north. Historic pre-Wyatt Wilton had only had two fronts, south (garden) and east (entrance).[3]

Wyatt's achievement had been to reorganise and replan the building to make a spacious north forecourt and symmetrical north entrance front for the first time, comfortable family rooms including a large new dining room and an informal west-facing library-living room (the *sine qua non* of Regency house planning); dozens of new bedrooms; and the Gothic Cloisters round the central quadrangle, which transformed the internal communications. Wyatt's Cloisters, "stately and very light" with plaster vaults by Francis Bernasconi, were on the whole admired and were therefore retained in 1913.[4] Most of Wyatt's other Gothic work at Wilton, however, was to be redressed according to twentieth-century neo-Georgian taste, though keeping Wyatt's well-considered plan which has enabled the place to function properly as a comfortable country house down to the present day.

The Pembrokes chose Warre as their architect. He was the fourth son of the provost of Eton, a keen oar, and later a Balliol friend of the writer Hilaire Belloc. Warre had been a school contemporary of Lord Pembroke, and his architectural career working mainly for Etonian clients started auspiciously.

After Oxford, Warre had trained as an architect in the office of Sir Thomas Graham Jackson (1835–1924), best known for his late nineteenth-century work at the university. Warre entered Jackson's architectural office in 1898 and adopted Jackson's eclectic classical/Tudor style and interest in building restoration.[5] In 1906, he succeeded Jackson as consultant architect to Eton College, a nepotistic role he filled until his father's retirement as provost in 1918. Warre restored the fifteenth-century

The entrance porch on the north front was designed to replace Wyatt's by Edmond Warre in 1913 for Reginald, 15th Earl of Pembroke. The Doric columns echo those of Sir William Chambers's Triumphal Arch opposite. The large coat of arms over the entrance impales Herbert with Paget for Lord Pembroke and his wife, Beatrice, sister of the 6th Marquess of Anglesey.

above The north front as remodelled by Edmond Warre. James Wyatt's Gothic windows were replaced with Tudor-style mullions, and his battlements gave way to a classical stone balustrade similar to those on the south and east fronts. Wyatt's *porte cochère* was demolished and replaced with a more impressive arrangement, still incorporating the panel of Henry VIII's arms.

cloisters at Eton, being responsible for the large brick buttress supporting Lupton's Tower, and the removal of the Georgian iron railings on the west side. He also remodelled the Provost's Lodge, installing central heating, building a new back stairs and generally de-Victorianizing, at a cost of £2,000 in 1910–14. He also carried out work in various schoolhouses, designed the Baldwin and Austen-Leigh Institute in 1911 and refenestrated the museum in Queen's Schools in 1913.

After the First World War, in which he served as a captain in the King's Royal Rifles, Warre repaired the Upper Schools at Eton, restoring stonework with the advice of the Society for the Protection of Ancient Buildings, and creating the choir room next to the chapel as a war memorial. Apart from this work at Eton, Warre had been involved at various country houses, including the restoration of Askerton in Cumberland for the Carlisle family and Beaudesert in Staffordshire for the 6th Marquess of Anglesey (Lord Pembroke's brother-in-law). He also built a church,

St. Martin, Edmonton, in North London, which was paid for by a school friend's mother, Mrs. Elizabeth Mason, in 1909.[6] He therefore seemed a very suitable architect for Lord Pembroke to choose for the proposed works he had in mind.

The first priority for reconstruction at Wilton in 1913 was Wyatt's symmetrical north front. The flanking towers, as remodelled by Thomas, the 8th Earl, were kept, but the early nineteenth-century Gothic *porte cochère* and battlements were demolished, and the whole façade refenestrated and newly detailed in an idiosyncratic Italianate-Tudor style somewhat reminiscent of Warre's old master, Sir Thomas Graham Jackson, in Oxford. It adds a new but harmonious dimension to the architecture of the house.

The most original part of Warre's remodelling is the new entrance porch that replaced James Wyatt's *porte cochère*. The new composition is both more welcoming and much grander than the previous incarnation. At first glance, all seems

following pages The north forecourt, looking from the house over the memorial garden and fountain to the Chambers Triumphal Arch and flanking Wyatt lodges. The 1970 formal design enhances the long rectangular layout of Wyatt's forecourt.

"Tudorbethan", but the central balustraded balcony supported on strong paired consoles carved with fierce eagles and lions is more Italianate. The Roman Doric columns framing the entrance echo those in Sir William Chambers's triumphal arch opposite, ingeniously linking Georgian academic neoclassicism and Warre's Edwardian bravura.

This sort of architecture has long been out of fashion. Even Christopher Hussey (editor of *Country Life*) opined: "While more attractive [than Wyatt], and providing a stately background to the forecourt ... [it] cannot be said to have risen completely to the opportunity, nor to the comparisons presented."[7] This seems unduly harsh. Warre's front is a clever introduction to the complex architectural glory of Wilton. It is sensitive to and subtly reflective of established elements of the place, and is in the way of an architectural summation of the history of the house, like the overture to an opera.

Inside the house, a similar sensitive approach was adopted. Wyatt's entrance hall of 1809 was simplified mainly by the loss of the display of the 1st Earl's trophy armour for which it had been designed. The armour was sent off to auction, and the wall brackets and shelves that supported it removed. This was partly to pay for the continuing construction work. Although war had broken out in 1914, most of the builders and craftsmen were too old to fight and carried on with their work, despite the suddenly changed and more stringent circumstances. Lady Pembroke ran a military hospital in part of the house, and Lord Pembroke and Warre joined their respective regiments in Flanders and northern France. The war, and the troubles in Ireland, had a significant impact on the family finances, leaving Lord Pembroke with a reduced income to pay for the works on which he had embarked optimistically in 1913.

Work during the war years concentrated on remodelling Wyatt's dining room, west of the entrance hall. The room was thought to be gloomy as well as hideous.[8] It was decided to bring it into harmony with the Jones-Webb rooms, a decision reinforced by the discovery of a cache of fittings, including joinery, chimneypieces and a magnificent pair of carved caryatids. The parts were assumed to be Jones's, thrown out by Wyatt. Although of splendid quality, these items are more likely to be eighteenth-century Jones Revival fittings from the 8th Earl's time, carefully saved during Wyatt's adaptations. The caryatids may have come from the 8th Earl's vestibule, attributed to John James of Greenwich. A pair of these and a heraldic pediment were used for the entrance doorway, which was moved from the corner to the centre of the south side of the dining room, to improve the layout of the room.

A large, pedimented, cartouched and swagged marble chimneypiece, possibly from the 8th Earl's hall, replaced Wyatt's simpler Gothic version. The proportions of the room were improved by lowering the ceiling and inserting a floor of bedrooms above. These were part of a modernisation that included the installation of twenty new bathrooms for guests and staff, described by Sidney Pembroke in his architectural notes. Previously there had been only one fixed, plumbed bathroom – for the king.

The Dining Room with caryatid doorcase. Wyatt's unfashionably bleak Gothic interior was remodelled during the First World War to bring it into line stylistically with the seventeenth-century state rooms, and introducing historic elements that had been stored since the 11th Earl's reconstruction of the north wing. The original green colour scheme was restored in 2010 by Lord and Lady Pembroke.

previous pages The Dining Room, redesigned by Edmond Warre in 1914, is an atmospheric Edwardian interior redolent of twentieth-century, neo-Georgian taste. The Inigo Jones–style marble chimneypiece, found in storage, was probably from the 8th Earl's Great Hall. The old Flemish tapestries were hung here, and the wall panels arranged to fit them. Warre designed the gilt frames for the two large portraits by Joshua Reynolds and the pair of "William Kent" side tables flanking the door.

Oswald Birley, portrait of Reginald, 15th Earl of Pembroke in Household Cavalry uniform. He was responsible for employing Edmond Warre to "de-Wyattise" the north side of the house.

The new Dining Room ceiling was coved and embellished with moulded plaster, and the walls were articulated with plaster panels to frame a set of three seventeenth-century Flemish tapestries found rolled up under the Library blind boxes. The Dining Room decoration could not be completed until after 1918. Warre had intended plentiful gilding and wanted an elaborate overmantel to frame the portrait of Lord Pembroke above the chimneypiece, but this had to be abandoned due to wartime price inflation and taxes, not to mention the loss of the Pembrokes' Irish estates' revenue, as revolution and civil war unfolded in that unhappy island.

The room was more cheaply finished in 1920 in dark "Georgian green" and white with no additional mouldings or gilding. To save money the cornice moulding was painted in *trompe l'oeil* and with such skill that it still deceives the eye today. Despite these final economies, Warre's Dining Room is nevertheless a handsome achievement, and was given additional authenticity by incorporating the caryatid doorcase, marble chimneypiece and old tapestries. The two large Reynolds portraits of Henry, the 10th Earl, and his wife, Elizabeth, were hung there, and Warre designed new gilded frames for them, and a pair of side tables to go underneath in the style of William Kent, who was then thought to have worked at Wilton. It is now known,

however, that everything in the house once attributed to Kent was actually carried out by the 9th Earl of Pembroke, or came to Wilton from Wanstead House in the 1820s.

Between the wars, attention turned to taming Wyatt's Gothic Library, which filled nearly the whole of the west wing facing the garden. This was an ugly-duckling twin to the old Dining Room with a grained coffered stucco ceiling. There were ante-rooms at either end. The one at the north end was divided off by a large moulded plaster arch, and the one to the south by tall double doors with Gothic panels. The walls were lined with oak-grained, crenellated timber bookcases with wire doors. The impetus for change here came when part of James Wyatt's ceiling fell down, precipitated by the impromptu widening of the room during building in 1804, when extra bits of wood had been tacked on to the ends of the roof beams.

The opportunity was therefore taken to remodel the room in 1933. A family "committee of taste" – which included Lady Pembroke, her brother Lord Anglesey

The South Ante Library. Wyatt's Gothic interior was simplified and classicised in 1933. It was redecorated in 2018 by David Mlinaric, and is arranged as a cabinet of Old Master drawings collected mainly by the 8th Earl, still in their original black and gold frames. The oval marble relief, after William Hoare of Bath's drawing of the 10th Earl as a boy, is by Peter Scheemakers, 1744.

Rex Whistler, painting of Wilton House from the south, 1933. Whistler was a friend of the family and regularly stayed at Wilton, where Edith Olivier, daughter of the former rector of Wilton, lived in the park's Daye House (T. H. Wyatt's dairy) and was a close friend and confidante. The painting captures the spirit of Wilton between the wars, when the house enjoyed an Indian summer, frequented by talented writers and artists, such as Rex Whistler, Cecil Beaton, Siegfried Sassoon and Stephen Tennant.

and her sons Sidney and David Herbert, along with their artist friend Rex Whistler (1905–1944), oversaw the proposals. The room was redesigned in the classical manner, with a plain plaster ceiling and giant Doric wall pilasters and cornice. The entrances to the anterooms at each end were replaced with magnificent new doorcases using two pairs of carved wooden caryatids from the sawmill, including one from the doorcase in the Dining Room, which was copied, at the same time the crenellations and wire doors were removed from the bookcases, which were painted cream. Without the trimmings, their good proportions could be appreciated. Whistler, with his pronounced architectural tastes, advised on all this, chose the cream-and-gold colour scheme and designed the new Doric wall pilasters himself. Rex Whistler was a regular visitor at Wilton and painted a characteristic view of the house with the Palladian Bridge, which is a twentieth-century pendant to the Wilsons, commissioned by Henry, the 10th Earl in the 1750s. Whistler was a huge fan

[234]

of the eighteenth century and a decorative designer of genius, as well as a talented painter, trained at the Slade School of Art in London.

The Library at Wilton is a rare three-dimensional neo-Georgian exercise by Whistler, and ranks beside his *trompe l'oeil* painted dining room at Plas Newydd, executed for Lord Anglesey at the same date, and his work for Edith Olivier, daughter of the rector of Wilton, who lived in the converted dairy cottage, renamed the Daye House, located in Wilton's park. Miss Olivier was a cultivated encourager and mother figure in Whistler's life.

The Second World War at Wilton, as at so many English houses, caused a huge upheaval. Most of the place was requisitioned by the army in 1940, and the contents hurriedly removed and stored. Sidney Herbert, later the 16th Earl, wrote in his architectural notes: "All this was heart-breaking. The empty rooms were used as offices... The old house withdrew into itself, and lost its charm, tho' outside not its beauty."[9] Not only were all the contents removed, some never to be replaced, but considerable damage was done to the fabric of the house by heavy military usage. Wyatt's ceiling over the Gothic Stairs collapsed. The edges of the stone treads of the stairs were broken by rolling a steel safe down them. Damp and rot affected the decoration of the seventeenth-century state rooms, making extensive postwar restoration work necessary.

Much of the effort in the decade after 1945 was directed at repairing war damage, such as eradicating dry rot in the Cube Rooms caused by the army blocking a vital internal downpipe with telephone wires, and replacing James Wyatt's collapsed ceiling over the Gothic Stairs with a plain coved affair after the original was brought down with a crash due to the stamping of military feet and the slamming of doors. Despite this "knocking around", the wartime occupation of the house by the army and its use as a military headquarters – GOC Southern Command – added a notable dimension to the history of the house. The Double Cube Room was used as a meeting room by the commanders of the Allied forces, and the D-Day landings were partly planned in that room. Both British and American troops were based at Wilton, and Lord and Lady Pembroke held a garden party there every year for the military "top brass" and their visitors.

In 1947, Sidney Herbert recorded with horror the damage in the state rooms:

On the north wall, between the fireplace and the Double Cube room wall, I could see where the ceiling was discoloured, and the white plaster showed; but immediately below it, in the carved wood cornice, I noticed something far worse, and could not believe my eyes ... fungus ... two large pieces projecting like loaves of brown bread. I fetched my father from the Library, and together we looked at the panelling, which had split, and when we touched it, large pieces crumbled into dust. Yet none of the soldiers or civilians using this room for the past eight years had noticed anything wrong. I telephoned the War Office and Ministry of Works the next morning, Monday and the Camp Commandant and others at Wilton were informed ... The War Office accepted responsibility for the damage (they could not do otherwise as the State rooms were still used by them), but wisely decided that it was a matter beyond their capabilities and

following pages The Library in the west wing. Wyatt's Gothic interior was redesigned in 1933, after part of the ceiling fell down, the delayed result of the impromptu widening of the room in 1804, when the roof joists were extended by tacked-on pieces of wood. The classical remodelling was supervised by a "committee of taste", comprising Lady Pembroke, her sons Sidney and David Herbert, her brother Lord Anglesey, and Rex Whistler. Whistler designed the Doric pilasters and suggested the cream-and-gold colour scheme for the bookcases, which were simplified by the removal of Wyatt's miniature crenellations. The room was decorated by John Fowler in 1963, with a hand-blocked Coles wallpaper and swagged curtains.

handed over the whole repair work to the Ministry of Works. Their best experts on decoration and architecture, and those who knew most about dry rot were called in, and every section of the walls and ceilings of the Single and Double Cube rooms were photographed and measured. The whole of the panelling between the fireplace and the Double Cube room door from floor to ceiling, was then cut away, as it was riddled with dry rot. An area about six feet square of the ceiling above had also to be cut away, and to do this a section of the flat lead roof had to be rolled back, a temporary roof fixed over it, and the coved plaster and wood sections of the ceiling cut away from behind.

It was then found that the dry rot had travelled eastwards into the Double Cube panelling, as well as through two or three feet of brick and stone into the Bachelor's Row bedrooms and bathrooms below and into the Anti-Library and Cloisters to the North. Much of this stone and brick had to be removed altogether. In doing so, two or three of the lovely rose coloured brick arches of the Tudor Inner quadrangle were revealed, and on a stone of the interior wall of the old house was found a mason's mark which proved to be the same as one found on a stone in Westminster Hall, which shows that one of the masons who helped to construct that Hall also assisted in the building of Wilton Abbey. Having removed all affected panelling, stonework and brickwork, the walls were treated with a strong anti-fungus solution, and every brick and stone and piece of mortar subjected to blow-lamps twice over, so that no infection could remain. The whole area was then left exposed to the air for a year ...

Inigo Jones and Webb had used pine panelling; the Ministry of Works obtained seasoned pine from Canada, and this was cut and carved by their own workmen and the firm of Fry and Sons from Frome in Somerset, who did the majority of the work. The panelling was then put in position, the new section of cornice carved ... and when fixed, the elaborate swags of fruit and flowers, palm leaves and other forms of decoration which had fortunately escaped to a large extent the dry rot ... were put back in position. The layers of gold leaf with which they were covered had largely protected them ... The work of restoration was beautifully done, and no praise can be too great for the Ministry of Works officials who supervised it, and for the firm of Fry who carried it out.[10]

As soon as he inherited Wilton on the death of his father in 1960, Sidney, as the 16th Earl, who loved Wilton and had long nurtured plans for its improvement, embarked on a complete redecoration and rearrangement of most of the interior, spending the large sum of £33,000 in four years. The renovation of the rooms was done with the advice of the fashionable London decorator John Fowler (1906–1977), and his American-born partner, Mrs. Nancy Lancaster (1897–1994). Wilton was one of their major jobs during the 1960s and one of the best surviving, fully revealing their talents. John Fowler was noted for his combination of artistic flair combined with historical knowledge of eighteenth-century decoration. Wyatt's Cloisters were repainted in shades of warm ochre or terracotta stippled over a yellow ground. Eighteenth-century pictures were then hung on the walls in place of the Regency arrangement of Roman sculpture that had been dismantled during the war. Originally the Cloisters had been finished in "fresco" by Francis Bernasconi, Wyatt's stuccoist, to look like ashlar stone blocks, but this had darkened, flaked and been damaged by damp. The warm Roman ochre was a good substitute, and provided the perfect background for the antique sculpture, when the Wyatt-Westmacott arrangements were later reassembled by William, the present 18th Earl of Pembroke in 2009–12.

The remodelling of the Library was also completed by Sidney in the 1960s by sashing the windows, gilding the cornice and doorcases, marbling the plinths of the pilasters and covering the walls with a specially printed large-pattern Coles paper in yellow and grey. A large marble Jonesian chimneypiece, from the stewards' room downstairs, was brought upstairs and installed here to complete the neo-Georgian ensemble.

The former Chinese Breakfast Room on the ground floor, designed by Sir Jeffry Wyatville in 1814, was made into the main dining room, close to the new kitchen, when the whole of the service side was reorganised and concentrated on the lower floor of the west wing. Wyatt's large kitchen was given up after the war, and is now used for shoot lunches. The original blue-ground Chinese wallpaper (destroyed by the army) in the new dining room was copied by hand in Hong Kong in 1960 at a cost of £550. Lady Pembroke's sitting room on the first floor of the East Gatehouse was also transformed – ugly Victorian bookshelves and the "Tudorbethan" overmantel put in by Elizabeth à Court, Lord Herbert of Lea's wife, were removed and a plain plaster ceiling with coved cornice installed. The walls were lined with white-painted panelling from the old housekeeper's room "to which Wyatt had banished it", and another of the 9th Earl's Jonesian marble chimneypieces was moved to the room, retrieved from elsewhere.

Much of the 16th Earl's work at Wilton was in the nature of decoration, but he also made one significant alteration to the external architecture. This was the replacement of Wyatt's decaying slate-hung Gothic clock turret on the East Gatehouse with a classical cupola of his own design, helped by C. A. Austen, the clerk of works, and a "man from the Ministry". Lord Pembroke was inspired by the form of the original cupola shown in an ink sketch on the estate survey of 1565, which had a standard Tudor half-onion profile. But Lord Pembroke's new cupola of 1963 is an octagonal *tempietto* with Tuscan columns, classical cornice and elegantly curved dome, more akin to Georgian stable clocks. It is a perfect addition to the house, and completes the Wilton skyline with a triumphant 1960s classical flourish. The new cupola incorporates the eighteenth-century clock made by Davis of Windsor for Henry, the 9th Earl, in 1745, the faces painted blue and gold, the traditional colours for public clocks in England.

The 1960s phase, when Sidney, the 16th Earl, aided by John Fowler, tied all the disparate Wilton threads together, reflects the continuing traditionalist strand in English twentieth-century architecture. It completed the move away from the Gothic style that had been initiated in 1913. Much of the 16th Earl's decoration by John Fowler survives, especially in the Cloisters, Library, Hunting Room and Chinese Breakfast Room. After his father's death in 1969 Henry, 17th Earl of Pembroke, kept the interior much as it was, but embarked on a major restoration of the fabric in the late 1980s and 1990s. The cloister roofs were rebuilt, the south front underpinned, leadwork renewed and much stonework repaired. Work began in 1987 under the

left Portrait of William, 18th Earl of Pembroke and 15th Earl of Montgomery, by Adrian Gottlieb, 2010. William inherited in 2003.

right Portrait of the Countess of Pembroke, by Rupert Alexander, 2018. Lord Pembroke married Victoria Bullough in 2010.

direction of the specialist conservation architects Purcell Miller Tritton, and was completed in 1992. The project enabled a thorough structural investigation of the fabric that led to discovering more of the surviving medieval and Tudor fabric and revealed the impact of the 1646 fire in the south front; this provided much new information, incorporated in this book. Stone repairs and conservation have continued since the completion of the major building phase; the Wells Cathedral architects Caroe and Partners replaced Purcell as architects in 2000, and much of the masonry repairs had been done by the former Cathedral Works masons from Salisbury led by Nicholas Durnan. The Palladian Bridge, Images Bridge, Saw Mill Bridge, Triumphal Arch, Holbein Porch, Tudor heraldic carving and the battlements on Wyatt's North Forecourt walls have been cleaned and repaired over the last twenty years in a continuous phased programme, initiated by Henry, 17th Earl of Pembroke, who also secured the future of the house by establishing the Wilton House charitable trust for the property's maintenance, and opening to public visitors.[11]

The present Lord Pembroke, William 18th Earl, inherited from his father at the age of twenty-five in 2003. He married Victoria Bullough in 2010, and they have worked together to restore the interiors more closely to their historic appearance, refurbishing the furniture and redisplaying the art collections, closer to their appearance before the military occupancy during the Second World War. The Warre Dining Room on the north front had been given up after the war and had become a general storage place and games room, stripped of its fittings, with the walls painted white, and dangling neon tube lights. Immediately after their marriage, the Pembrokes restored this room to its original appearance, with the assistance of David Mlinaric (b. 1939), the leading English decorator, who has advised on many historic houses including Beningbrough, Waddesdon and Spencer House, as well as public buildings such as London's Royal Opera House, National Gallery and Victoria and Albert Museum. Though now partly retired, Mlinaric continues to act as consultant for special historic interiors and has been closely involved, for instance, in the major refurbishment of Chatsworth for the Duke of Devonshire. At Wilton as a friend of Lord Pembroke's family, he was happy to advise on the decoration, beginning with the Dining Room where the walls have been repainted the original dark blue-green, but with gilding now added, as had been intended but not executed in order to economise in 1919, following the First World War.

All the furniture, tapestries and pictures have been reinstated where they were originally placed. As a north-facing, rather dark room it has been enhanced by mirror glass panels between the windows, and new crimson silk curtains have been hung there. The sculptural decoration was restored by Stephen Pettifer of Coade Ltd., a tenant in the sawmill yard on the estate, who has revived the Georgian technique of making Coade Stone, a frost-proof terracotta. Having trained at the City & Guilds of London Art School, and after working as a sculptor and restorer, Pettifer established his Coade studio at Wilton in 2000. He has played an important role in much of the recent work at Wilton. In the Dining Room, for instance, the pair of seventeenth-century-style gilt wood chandeliers was handled by him using one original and copying the other. He also reproduced the eighteenth-century caryatids

The Chinese Breakfast Room, designed by Jeffry Wyatville in Brighton Pavilion taste in 1814. The Chinese wallpaper was copied in Hong Kong in 1963, as part of a redecoration by John Fowler, who designed the curtains.

on either side of the doorcase. Coade Ltd. is one of a number of specialist businesses and art studios now occupying converted buildings in the sawmill yard, typical of late twentieth-century economic diversification on modern English landed estates.

Stephen Pettifer's most important contribution to Wilton has been in the brilliant reassemblage of the 8th Earl's classical sculpture in Wyatt's Cloisters, where the Coade studio, equipment, staff and expertise made it possible to achieve the whole ambitious scheme as an "in-house" project. The sculpture survived *in situ* in its early nineteenth-century Westmacott and Wyatt arrangement until the Second World War and the army's requisition of the place as its headquarters in 1940. The Cloisters were then divided into stenographers' offices, with hardboard partitions, and the sculpture was removed from the south, west and east sides. The more important busts were stored in the Riding School but all the largest pieces including the marble statues, sarcophagi and stone plinths were scattered over the grounds. Even James Wyatt's two chimneypieces supported on antique black "porphyry" columns were dismantled. The columns were subsequently sold with other "surplus" marble and statuary at a sale on the premises organised by Christie's in 1962.

Many of the display arrangements had been designed by Westmacott in the form of timber stands painted to simulate stone and incorporating sculptural reliefs. These wooden structures did not survive hasty dismantling and were lost. After the war there was no question of reinstating the sculpture because of its weight, and the cost involved, and also prevailing fashions. English collections of classical sculpture, which were largely Roman copies of Greek originals or Renaissance copies of Roman works, were then generally despised by the English art establishment, especially the experts at the British Museum with their post-Elgin love of Greek art. That attitude led to the loss of many eighteenth-century collections of ancient sculpture from British country houses in the second half of the twentieth century.

When Sidney, 16th Earl, reinstated and decorated the Wilton interiors in the 1960s, there was no enthusiasm for restoring the sculpture galleries, and he contented himself with displaying selected busts along the sides of the Cloisters as redecorated by John Fowler. The 8th Earl's sculpture collection with its extraordinary historical associations was forgotten, the important sarcophagi were used as flower pots in the garden and other pieces gradually engulfed in the shrubbery. The revival of interest in English sculpture collections was sparked in the 1980s by the University of Cologne's publication of a series of catalogues of eighteenth-century English Grand Tour collections of antiquities. The Cologne team from Germany searched and photographed what pieces were still at Wilton at that time. Further investigations revealed more, including a fourth-century BC Greek funerary relief propped up in the clock turret, as well as items buried in the building yard which had to be re-excavated as if by Piranesi or Jenkins in the eighteenth-century Campagna. When it was clear that there was enough surviving at Wilton of the 8th Earl's collection to re-create the antique sculpture display on all four sides of Wyatt's Cloisters, Lord Pembroke and the estate's trustees made the decision to undertake this project in 2007 and most of the work was carried out in 2009–12.

The chimneypiece in the East Cloister was removed during military occupation of the house during the Second World War, when the Cloisters were used for stenographers' offices. It was restored in 2012. The Triptolemus sarcophagus dating from AD 170 was reinstated as intended by Wyatt. It is the most important item in the collection of Roman sculpture.

above and opposite above The East Cloister, with the classical sculpture arrangement, including busts from the Mazarin Collection and three sarcophagi from the Via Appia catacomb, restored. The two tall, fluted "peacock columns" of antique Pavonazzo marble are reputed to come from the Arundel Collection. They were in the 8th Earl's entrance vestibule in the eighteenth century.

opposite below The bay window in the East Cloister. The large seated statue of Ceres displayed here was sold with other sculpture in 1961 and is one of a number of the 8th Earl's pieces which have recently been reacquired as part of the restoration of the Cloisters.

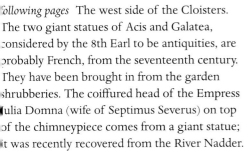

following pages The west side of the Cloisters. The two giant statues of Acis and Galatea, considered by the 8th Earl to be antiquities, are probably French, from the seventeenth century. They have been brought in from the garden shrubberies. The coiffured head of the Empress Julia Domna (wife of Septimus Severus) on top of the chimneypiece comes from a giant statue; it was recently recovered from the River Nadder.

above The south Cloisters. The marble copies of the much admired *Apollo Belvedere* and the *Venus de' Medici* are by the English neoclassical sculptor Joseph Wilton and were commissioned from him in Rome in 1760 by the 10th Earl. Wyatt's pedestals contain outlets for his pioneering hot-air central heating system.

above right The south Cloisters looking west.

right The north-east corner, reinstated to Wyatt's proposal. The sarcophagus from the Via Appia contains a portrait of the couple interred, and wild animals.

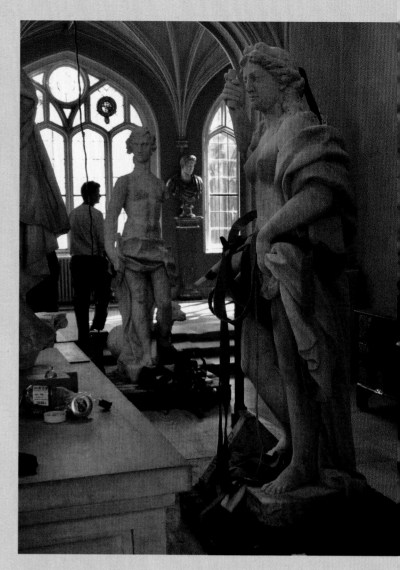

opposite Statues being restored for reinstatement in the house. Acis and Galatea after conservation, being brought back and installed in the West Cloister by the team from Coade Stone, whose workshop is on the estate and whose expertise and equipment made it possible to carry out the whole sculpture restoration programme as an in-house job.

right Carved Roman fountain in the form of a bearded face. Rescued in a mossy state from the garden, and after conservation by Coade. It is now displayed in the south-east corner of the Cloisters.

below right Conservation in progress in the Coade workshop, washing with ionised water. Bacchus in the background has been conserved.

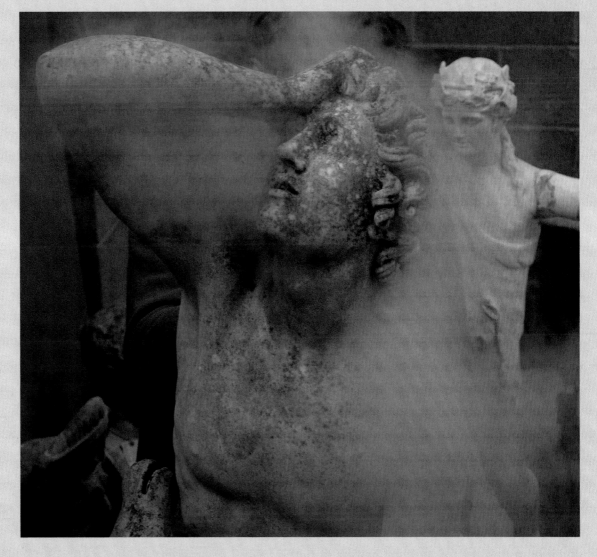

The North Ante Library. This
pendant to the South Ante Library,
de-Wyattised at the same time in
1933, has recently been redecorated
by David Mlinaric and arranged
as a Grand Tour–type cabinet
of small Old Master paintings,
recovered from storage and
restored, and recent acquisitions,
including two views of Vesuvius
by Antonio Joli (Canaletto's
master), acquired by Henry, 17th
Earl of Pembroke.

Stephen Pettifer was able to move all the heavy pieces, and clean and conserve
them. In his studio, he replaced rusted iron cramps with stainless steel, and then
lifted them with specialist tackle into their chosen places in the house. He reinstated both Wyatt's fireplaces, using black Kilkenny marble from Ireland for the
columns, as the centrepieces of the east and west Cloisters, and he made new
stone plinths for several of the statues matching those of Wyatt's and Westmacott's that still survived. He also made outdoor copies of some pieces, to continue
their role as garden ornaments, after the originals were brought inside for conservation reasons. The Wyatt Gothic corbels round the walls had never been used
and were removed in 1962. Only one was retained, to support the fire alarm, and
a mould was taken from this to reinstate the corbels on all four sides of the Cloisters. They are an important part of Wyatt's architectural design, helping to "pace"
the walls and provide a link between the sculpture display and Bernasconi's stucco

vaults above. So once again, the oldest surviving collection of antique – Greek and Roman – statuary in an English country house can be admired in its historically inspired arrangement, and as an essential part of Wyatt's design for the Cloisters. To quote Dr. Gustav Waagen (director of the National Gallery in Berlin) when he visited Wilton in the 1840s: "The visitor may fancy himself at once transported to Italy for the large collection of sculpture is arranged in this gallery with great attention to picturesque effect".[12]

Some of the picture collection has also been redisplayed. The north and south ante-libraries have become "cabinets" for displays of paintings and Italian drawings, against a dark picture-gallery-red chosen by David Mlinaric. In the state rooms, the oak boards have been repaired and appropriate rugs put down. The new rug in the Double Cube, measuring 48 feet by 22 feet, was handwoven in Afghanistan using vegetable dyes and a seventeenth-century Persian design. The theatrical crimson silk velvet curtains with elaborate passementerie and tassels designed by Richard Westmacott in 1824 for the Single and Double Cube Room windows have been reproduced to the archive design. The old ones had decayed from sun damage over nearly two hundred years. Authentic silk velvet was acquired from Lyon in France. In the Colonnade Room a state bed has been copied from a seventeenth-century example at Knole and installed in the bed alcove under David Mlinaric's direction, emphasising the historical function of the room. In the Corner Rooms the original crimson flock paper, hung by Catherine Woronzow in 1811, has been reproduced in replica by Watts of Westminster, as a background to the best small Flemish and Italian paintings in the collection, which have also been cleaned and relit to show them to their best advantage. In the Gothic Hall, the walls and Bernasconi's stucco vault have been repainted a stone colour as intended by Wyatt, and Richard Wilson's landscapes placed there, as they were in the nineteenth century. The Smoking Rooms were rehung with moiréed silk in 2017, yellow in the large and green watered silk in the small; silk hangings were intended by the 9th Earl but had been replaced with paint in the economising twentieth century. These improvements have also been undertaken with David Mlinaric's advice, working closely with Lady P.[13]

As it stands in the third decade of the twenty-first century, Wilton is a remarkable achievement. It is one of only a few places in the world (many of them in England) that combine great architecture, an unblemished landscape setting and private art collections of highest quality after nearly five centuries in the ownership of a single family. It is a historic entity moreover which today is maintained in glorious condition and arranged with informed knowledge, taste and visual panache. Successive generations of the Pembroke family in the twentieth century, despite wars, revolutions, cultural and economic disasters, and socialism, have by their determined endeavours and "lifetimes given in devotion", not only held all this together, but have enhanced and improved it and also enabled it to flourish and inspire a new century and new generations with some of the finest artistic achievements from the English past. Wilton remains as it was in the eighteenth century, one of the great showplaces of England, and is open to the public every summer, as well as continuing to serve as the family home of the Earls of Pembroke and Montgomery.

Notes and References

Introduction *pages 24–39*

1 Tresham Lever, *The Herberts of Wilton* (London: John Murray, 1967), 101.
2 Peter Stewart, *A Catalogue of the Sculpture Collection at Wilton House* (Oxford: Archaeopress, 2020).
3 James Kennedy, *A Description of the Antiquities and Curiosities in Wilton House* (Salisbury: E. Easton, 1767).
4 British Library. Cotton MS. Faust. B. III. Published, 1830: Richard Colt Hoare and W. H. Black, eds., *Chronicon Vilodunense*.
5 VCH, *Wiltshire*, III (1956), 231–42.
6 W.A.M. I, 248–56; John Harvey, ed., *William Worcester Itineraries* (Oxford: Clarendon, 1969).
7 John Heywood, 'The Restoration of the South Front of Wilton House: The Development of the House Reconsidered', *Architectural History* (Essex Record Office, 2002), 76–117.

Chapter One *pages 40–65*

1 Lever, op cit, 3–16.
2 Mark Girouard, 'The Development of Longleat House', *Archaeological Journal*, 116 (1959) 202–16.
3 'Survey of the Lands of William Earl of Pembroke', WRO 2057/53; C. R. Straton, ed., *Survey of the 1st Earl of Pembroke at Wilton House* (Oxford: Roxburghe Club, 1910).
4 Wiltshire Archaeological Survey, Devizes. J. C. Buckler watercolour, 1803, Yale Centre for British Art, Paul Mellon Coll. B1991.40.101. Watercolour of Holbein Porch 1804, signed 'J. Buckler'.
5 *Camden Miscellany*, Third Series 4 (1902), 'Journal of Sir Roger Wilbraham', 65.
6 John Britton, ed., *Aubrey's Natural History of Wiltshire* (London, 1847), 83.
7 Mark Girouard, *Elizabethan Architecture: Its Rise and Fall, 1540–1640* (London: Yale University Press for the Paul Mellon Centre for British Art, 2009).
8 NAL MS 1982.30. 'An inventorie of alle the beddes, hangings and all other householde stuff and armour etc., remayning at the mansion house of the right honourable Erle of Penbroke [sic] at Wilton aforesaid, primo Januarii anno Elizabethe Regine quarto' (1561).
9 *Camden Miscellany* XVI, Third Series 16 (1936), 66, 'Description of a journey made into the Westerne

Counties. Made by a Lieutenant of the Military Company in Norwich in 1635'.
10 Claude Blair, 'The Wilton "Montmorency" Armor: An Italian Armor to Henry VIII', *Metropolitan Museum Journal*, 38, 95–143.
11 Worcester College, Oxford. Isaac de Caux, design for chapel at Wilton House.
12 Heywood, op. cit.
13 *Camden Miscellany* XVI, op. cit.
14 Britton, op. cit.
15 Adam Nicolson, *Earls of Paradise: England: The Dream of Perfection* (London: Harper Press, 2008), 107–8.

Chapter Two *pages 66–115*

1 Howard Colvin, 'The South Front of Wilton House', *Essays in English Architectural History* (New Haven: Yale University Press, 1999).
John Summerson, *Inigo Jones* (London: Paul Mellon Centre for British Art, 2002).
Giles Worsley, *Inigo Jones and the European Classicist Tradition* (London: Paul Mellon Centre for British Art, 2007).
John Harris and Gordon Higgott, *Inigo Jones: Complete Architectural Drawings* (London: Sotheby Parke Bernet, 1989).
John Bold, *Wilton House and English Palladianism* (London: Her Majesty's Stationery Office, 1988).
Heywood, op. cit.
2 Daniel Defoe, *Tour thro' the whole island of Great Britain* (London, 1724–27), 3 vols.
3 A. A. Tait, 'Isaac de Caux and the South Front of Wilton House', *Burlington Magazine* CVI (1964), 74.
4 John Britton, ed., *Aubrey's Natural History of Wiltshire* (London, 1847), 83–86.
5 Colvin, op. cit., 181–90.
6 Roy Strong, *The Renaissance Garden in England* (London: Thames and Hudson, 1994), 122–23.
7 Celia Fiennes, *Through England on a Side Saddle* (London: Leadenhall Press, 1884), 4.
8 *Camden Miscellany* XVI, op. cit., 66.
9 John Taylor, *Wandering to see the Wonders of the West* (London, 1649); Matthew Dimmock, Andrew Hadfield, Margaret Healy eds., *The Intellectual Culture of the English

opposite A Japanese water garden was laid out immediately south-east of the Whispering Seat in the 1990s.

Country House 1500–1700 (Manchester University Press, 2018); Marta Straznicky, 'Case Study: Wilton House', 217–77.

10 Society of Antiquaries, Harley, 'Seats', 7, 47.

11 Britton, op. cit.

12 Colvin, op. cit., 189.

13 Rijksprentenkabinet, Amsterdam. Twelve etchings for Grotesque Panels by Pearce, 1647.

14 Britton, op. cit., 85.

15 Bainbridge Buckeridge, *Essay towards an English School of Painting* (London: Thomas Payne, 1706).

16 Gordon Higgott, 'Designs for Painted Decoration by Edward Pearce Senior'.

17 Wyatt office survey drawing *c.* 1802 showing the original arrangement of the panels. Pembroke Archives, Wiltshire Record Office.

18 Britton, op. cit.

19 Mireille Galinou, 'Painting the Chase', *Country Life*, 27 February 2013, 62–65.

20 Fiennes, op. cit.

21 Jean Barbet, *Livre d'Architecture, d'Autels et de Cheminées* (Paris, 1633).

22 Lorenzo Magalotti, *Travels of Cosmo, the Third, Grand Duke of Tuscany, through England during the reign of King Charles II* (London: J. Mawman, 1821), 150.

Chapter Three *pages 116–171*

1 Horace Walpole, *Anecdotes of Painting in England: With Some Account of the Principal Artists. Collected by the late George Vertue.* 4 vols. (1771), IV.

2 John Bold, op. cit.

3 Colvin; B. L. Harley Papers xlvi.

4 Peter Stewart, op. cit.

5 Lewis-Walpole Library, Yale University, George Vertue, Double Cube Room at Wilton House, pencil sketch *c.* 1740.

6 Tate Gallery Turner Bequest XLIV N.

7 Walpole Society, 'Vertue Note Books' V,130. The authorship of the Palladian Bridge has been much debated. Stephen Parissien surmised it was based on a lost sketch by Inigo Jones. DPhil Thesis, 'Roger Morris' Oxford (1989).

8 David Jacques, *Gardens of Court and Country: English Design 1630–1730* (New Haven: Yale University Press, 2017) 256–57.

9 Gustav Waagen, *Treasures of Art in Great Britain* (4 vols, London, 1854–57)

10 Ibid.

11 W.R.O., Wilton Archives

12 Sidney, 16th Earl of Pembroke, *Henry, Elizabeth and George, 10th Earl of Pembroke and his Circle* (1939).

13 John Harris, *Sir William Chambers* (1970).

14 W.R.O., Wilton Archives 2057/H1/3, Chambers' design 1760; H1/3 Chambers's Accounts.

15 Sidney, 16th Earl of Pembroke, op. cit.

16 *Historical Manuscripts Commission*, 9th Report, 380. Dr. Thomas Eyre to Lord Herbert in Vienna, 1 January 1779.

Chapter Four *pages 172–217*

1 John Martin Robinson, *James Wyatt 1746–1813: Architect to George III* (London: Paul Mellon Centre for Studies in British Art, 2013), 238–39.

2 Ibid. 305.

3 Wiltshire Record Office (WRO), Pembroke Archives 2057/H1/6, Wyatt-Pembroke correspondence.

4 Ibid. Benjamin Dean Wyatt to the 11th Earl of Pembroke, 13 April 1809.

5 WRO 2057/H1/6, Correspondence between 11th Earl of Pembroke and James Wyatt. Ibid.

6 WRO 2057/H1/9, Catherine Woronzow, Countess of Pembroke's Notebooks; 2057/H1/18, Westmacott's and Wyatt's drawings for Wilton.

7 WRO 2057/H1/6, Letter from the 11th Earl of Pembroke to Richard Westmacott, 27 July 1812; WRO 2057/H1/10, Wyatt's sculpture proposals annotated by Catherine Woronzow "Proposed arrangement of sculpture in the cloyster by Mr.Wyatt".

8 "Wansted House, Essex, Magnificent Furniture … which will be sold by Auction by Mr. Robins … on the premises on Monday 10 June 1822 and 3 following Days … London 1822." Lots 16–17, 25 June; Lot 12, 26 June; Lots 23–28, 2 July can be identified today at Wilton.

9 Tresham Lever, *The Herberts of Wilton*, op. cit.

Chapter Five *pages 218–253*

1 Wilton Estate Office, Sidney, the 16th Earl of Pembroke, 'Notes on Building Alterations… at Wilton House in the Twentieth Century', MS.

2 Bold, op. cit., 25–76.

3 Waagen, op. cit., 143.

4 Eton College Archives. Coll/06/4/58p91/35p318/785.

5 Ibid.

6 Christopher Hussey, 'James Wyatt and Wilton House', *Country Life*, 8 August, 1963, 314.

7 Pembroke 'Notes', op. cit.

8 Ibid.

9 Ibid.

10 Wilton Estate Office. Correspondence and accounts for restoration programme, 1988–2000.

11 Ibid., 2010–19.

The Earls of Pembroke

WILLIAM HERBERT, 1st Earl of Pembroke (1506–1570)
Created Earl of Pembroke 1551. Married in 1533 Anne Parr, sister of Catherine Parr, daughter of Sir Thomas Parr (d. 1552).

HENRY HERBERT, 2nd Earl of Pembroke (1534–1601)
Eldest son of the 1st Earl, inherited 1570. Married (3) in 1577 Mary Sidney (d. 1621).

WILLIAM HERBERT, 3rd Earl of Pembroke (1580–1630)
Eldest son of the 2nd Earl, inherited 1600. Married in 1577 Mary, daughter
of the 7th Earl of Shrewsbury (d. 1650).

PHILIP HERBERT, 4th Earl of Pembroke (1584–1650)
Brother of the 3rd Earl, inherited 1630. Created 1st Earl of Montgomery 1605.
Married (1) in 1604 Susan de Vere, daughter of the 17th Earl of Oxford (1587–1629).
Married (2) in 1630 Lady Anne Clifford, daughter of the Earl of Cumberland (d. 1676).

PHILIP HERBERT, 5th Earl of Pembroke – 2nd Earl of Montgomery (1621–1669)
Eldest son of the 4th Earl, inherited 1649. Married (1) in 1639 Penelope Naunton, daughter of Sir Robert Naunton
(1620–1647). Married (2) in 1649 Katherine Villiers, daughter of Sir William Villiers (d. 1678).

WILLIAM HERBERT, 6th Earl of Pembroke – 3rd Earl of Montgomery (1640–1674)
Eldest son of the 5th Earl, inherited 1669. Unmarried.

PHILIP HERBERT, 7th Earl of Pembroke – 4th Earl of Montgomery (1653–1683)
Half-brother of the 6th Earl, inherited 1674. Married Henriette de Quéroualle (d. 1728).

THOMAS HERBERT, 8th Earl of Pembroke – 5th Earl of Montgomery (1656–1733)
Brother of the 7th Earl, inherited 1683. Married (1) Margaret Sawyer in 1684, daughter of Sir Robert Sawyer (d. 1706). Married (2) 1708 Barbara Slingsby,
daughter of Sir Thomas Slingsby (d. 1722). Married (3) in 1725 Mary, daughter of 1st Viscount Howe (d. 1749).

HENRY HERBERT, 9th Earl of Pembroke – 6th Earl of Montgomery (1693–1750)
Eldest son of the 8th Earl, inherited 1733. Married in 1733 Mary Fitzwilliam, daughter of Viscount Fitzwilliam (1707–1769).

HENRY HERBERT, 10th Earl of Pembroke – 7th Earl of Montgomery (1734–1794)
Son of the 9th Earl, inherited 1750. Married in 1756 Lady Elizabeth Spencer, daughter of the 3rd Duke of Marlborough (1737–1831).

GEORGE HERBERT, 11th Earl of Pembroke – 8th Earl of Montgomery (1759–1827)
Son of the 10th Earl, inherited 1794. Married (1) in 1787 Elizabeth, daughter of Topham Beauclerk (d. 1793).
Married (2) in 1808 Catherine, Daughter of Count Simon Woronzow (d. 1856).

ROBERT HERBERT, 12th Earl of Pembroke – 9th Earl of Montgomery (1791–1862)
Eldest son of the 11th Earl, inherited 1827.

SIDNEY HERBERT, 1st Baron Herbert of Lea (1810–1861)
Half-brother of the 12th Earl. Married in 1846 Elizabeth à Court (1822–1911).

GEORGE ROBERT HERBERT, 13th Earl of Pembroke
– 10th Earl of Montgomery (1850–1895)
Eldest son of Lord Herbert of Lea, inherited 1862. Married in 1874
Lady Gertrude Talbot, daughter of the 18th Earl of Shrewsbury (1840–1906).

SIDNEY HERBERT, 14th Earl of Pembroke
– 11th Earl of Montgomery (1853–1913)
Brother of the 13th Earl, inherited 1895. Married in 1877
Lady Beatrix Lambton, daughter of the Earl of Durham (1859–1914).

REGINALD HERBERT, 15th Earl of Pembroke – 12th Earl of Montgomery (1880–1960)
Eldest son of the 14th Earl, inherited 1913. Married in 1904 Lady Beatrice Paget, daughter of Lord Alexander Paget, sister of the 6th Marquess of Anglesey (1883–1973).

SIDNEY HERBERT, 16th Earl of Pembroke – 13th Earl of Montgomery (1906–1969)
Eldest son of the 15th Earl, inherited 1960. Married in 1936 Lady Mary Hope, daughter of the 1st Marquess of Linlithgow (d. 1995).

HENRY HERBERT, 17th Earl of Pembroke – 14th Earl of Montgomery (1939–2003)
Son of the 16th Earl, inherited 1969. Married (1) in 1966 Claire Pelly. Married (2) in 1988 Miranda Juliet Oram.

WILLIAM HERBERT, 18th Earl of Pembroke – 15th Earl of Montgomery (b. 1978–)
Son of the 17th Earl, inherited 2003. Married in 2010 Victoria Bullough.

LADY ALEXANDRA HERBERT
(b. 2011)

REGINALD, LORD HERBERT
(b. 2012)

THE HON. LOUIS HERBERT
(b. 2014)

LADY BEATRICE HERBERT
(b. 2016)

Acknowledgements

The Earl and Countess of Pembroke

Tertius and Claire Murray Threipland, and the Wilton House Trustees

Chris Rolfe, Resident Agent at Wilton, Charlotte Spender, Nigel Bailey,
Tim Goodman, Stephen Pettifer of Coade Limited

My co-authors for the Wilton Trilogy, Peter Stewart and Francis Russell

Fellow historians Mark Girouard, John Goodall, Mary Miers, the late
Giles Worsley, Gordon Higgott, John Harris, Alexander Echlin, Julian Orbach

John d'Arcy and the staff of the Wiltshire Record Office, Kate Harris at Longleat,
the RIBA Drawings Collection, the librarian at the Society of Antiquaries,
the Bridgeman Art Library

The photographers who have taken the illustrations specially—the late
Paul Barker, Will Pryce, Simon Upton, Guido Petruccioli, Stephen Slater,
Ros Liddington and Dominic Brown

The following organisations for allowing reproduction of images: the RIBA
Drawings Collection, *Country Life Magazine*, the Wiltshire County Museum

Charles Miers and Jacob Lehman of Rizzoli, and Robert Dalrymple,
the designer

Index

First published in the United States of America in 2021 by
Rizzoli Electa, a Division of
Rizzoli International Publications, Inc.
300 Park Avenue South, New York, NY 10010
www.rizzoliusa.com

Publisher: Charles Miers
Editor: Jacob Lehman
Production Manager: Alyn Evans
Production Assistant: Olivia Russin
Managing Editor: Lynn Scrabis

All photography courtesy of the Wilton House Trust,
with grateful acknowledgement of the following: pages 2–3,
6–7, 16–17, 23, 38–39, 55, 76–77, 92, 94–95, 102, 111, 119, 130 (left),
162, 173, 186, 232, 236–237, 240 (left), 241 and 249 (below) © Will
Pryce; pages 4–5, 8–9, 10–11, 14–15, 18–19, 20, 32–33, 68–69, 75,
86–87, 98, 100, 101, 103, 104, 106–107, 108–109, 110, 112–113, 114,
115, 121, 136, 138–139, 140, 141, 142–143, 144, 147, 148–149, 150,
151, 153, 155, 156, 157, 170, 174–175, 176, 177, 181, 184–185, 191, 196,
197, 198 (below), 204 (left), 205, 206, 208, 213, 214, 222, 224–225,
226–227, 229, 230–231, 244, 245, 246–247, 248, 249 (above) and
254 © Simon Upton; pages 43, 56, 67, 71, 73, 105, 118 (above),
122, 123, 128, 129, 132, 133, 146, 158, 164, 165, 166, 167, 180 and
215 © Bridgeman Library; pages 92 and 94–95 © Country Life;
pages 64–65, 89, 90, 97, 127, 182, 192–193, 203, 209, 210 and 243
© Paul Barker; pages 219 and 234 © RIBA.

Dust jacket front © Simon Upton
Dust jacket back © Paul Barker

Typeset in Monotype Dante
Design by Dalrymple

Printed in China

2021 2022 2023 2024 / 10 9 8 7 6 5 4 3 2 1

ISBN: 978-0-8478-7007-3
Library of Congress Control Number: 2020948615

Facebook.com/RizzoliNewYork
Twitter: @Rizzoli_Books
Instagram.com/RizzoliBooks
Pinterest.com/RizzoliBooks
Youtube.com/user/RizzoliNY
Issuu.com/Rizzoli